MATH

5

Practice 101 Minutes Weekly to Master Your Math Skills

PRACTICE WORKBOOK 1

- ✓ **Advanced Addition and Subtraction**
- ✓ **Multiplication and Division**
- ✓ **Multiplication and Division Patterns**
- ✓ **Multiplication Properties**

101Minute.com

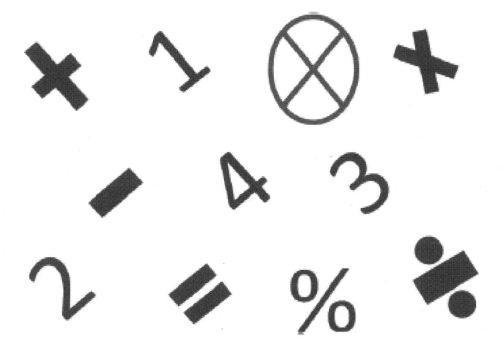

Ritesh Arora

About 101Minute.com

Welcome to 101Minute.com, a guide dedicated to help students excel academically.

We are focused on creating educational programs that help to enhance student's skills across various grades and subjects. Modules are designed per grade level that progressively enhances their skill and confidence each day.

Each subject category has several quizzes designed to assess student's mastery with the concept. By consistently devoting 101 minutes per week, students can demonstrate significant improvement.

We are committed to serving our student community by building effective tools and reward programs. We are open to receiving feedback on how we can improve to make this an even better experience for our students. Our goal is to create a fun and learning social educational environment for students, and reward them for their achievements.

Please visit us at 101Minute.com.

TABLE OF CONTENTS

1. MATHEMATICAL PROBLEMS USING EVEN AND ODD NUMBERS

1. Is 293 + 408 an odd or an even number?

2. Is 326 + 312 an odd or an even number?

3. Is 277 + 395 an odd or an even number?

4. Is 482 + 504 an odd or an even number?

5. Is 341 + 504 an odd or an even number?

6. Is 222 + 184 an odd or an even number?

7. Is 274 + 248 an odd or an even number?

8. Is 197 + 225 an odd or an even number?

9. Is 229 + 293 an odd or an even number?

10. Is 261 + 344 an odd or an even number?

11. Is 144 + 88 an odd or an even number?

12. Is 165 + 152 an odd or an even number?

13. Is 309 + 463 an odd or an even number?

14. Is 325 + 497 an odd or an even number?

15. Is 133 + 88 an odd or an even number?

16. Is 213 + 248 an odd or an even number?

17. Is 456 + 472 an odd or an even number?

18. Is 181 + 184 an odd or an even number?

19. Is 404 + 408 an odd or an even number?

20. Is 213 + 259 an odd or an even number?

21. Is 117 + 55 an odd or an even number?

22. Is 149 + 120 an odd or an even number?

23. Is 352 + 344 an odd or an even number?

24. Is 378 + 376 an odd or an even number?

25. Is 325 + 472 an odd or an even number?

26. Is 149 + 123 an odd or an even number?

27. Is 117 + 56 an odd or an even number?

28. Is 165 + 157 an odd or an even number?

29. Is 277 + 376 an odd or an even number?

30. Is 229 + 280 an odd or an even number?

31. Is 245 + 312 an odd or an even number?

32. Is 248 + 216 an odd or an even number?

33. Is 300 + 280 an odd or an even number?

34. Is 181 + 191 an odd or an even number?

35. Is 133 + 89 an odd or an even number?

36. Is 341 + 531 an odd or an even number?

37. Is 261 + 361 an odd or an even number?

38. Is 196 + 152 an odd or an even number?

39. Is 293 + 429 an odd or an even number?

40. Is 430 + 440 an odd or an even number?

2. NEGATIVE AND POSITIVE NUMBERS (SORTING ORDER)

1. Are -14, -17, -15 in ascending order?
    a) False
    b) True

2. Identify the right relationship to put numbers in order.

-1	is the middle number
-13	is the greatest number
-3	is the smallest number

3. Identify the right relationship to put numbers in order.

-6	is the middle number
-15	is the greatest number
-12	is the smallest number

4. Are 5, 9, -7 in ascending order?
    a) False
    b) True

5. Are -11, -1, 21 in descending order?
    a) False
    b) True

6. Are -29, -19, -9 in ascending order?
    a) True
    b) False

7. Identify the right relationship to put numbers in order.

-2	is the middle number
-19	is the greatest number
-15	is the smallest number

8. Are -30, -20, -10 in descending order?
    a) False
    b) True

9. Find the biggest number among -14, -12, -25.
    a) -12
    b) -14
    c) -25

10. Are -19, -9, -10 in descending order?
    a) False
    b) True

11. Are -5, -9, -7 in ascending order?
    a) False
    b) True

12. Are -17, -14, -10 in ascending order?
    a) True
    b) False

13. Are -5, -15, -10 in ascending order?
   a) False
   b) True

14. Find the biggest number among -4, -14, -24.
   a) -4
   b) -14
   c) -24

15. Are -15, -20, -25 in descending order?
   a) True
   b) False

16. Write a whole number between -20 and -18

17. Are -5, -9, -13 in descending order?
   a) True
   b) False

18. Are -9, -7, -5 in ascending order?
   a) True
   b) False

19. Are -29, -18, 14 in descending order?
   a) False
   b) True

20. Identify the right relationship to put numbers in order.
   -1   is the middle number
   -14   is the greatest number
   -4   is the smallest number

21. Are 5, 15, -10 in ascending order?
   a) False
   b) True

22. Are -26, -19, -13 in ascending order?
   a) True
   b) False

23. Identify the right relationship to put numbers in order.
   -15   is the middle number
   -19   is the greatest number
   -17   is the smallest number

24. Identify the right relationship to put numbers in order.
   -2   is the middle number
   -19   is the greatest number
   -14   is the smallest number

25. Are 1, -3, -5 in descending order?
   a) True
   b) False

26. Identify the right relationship to put numbers in order.
   -4   is the middle number
   -14   is the greatest number
   -8   is the smallest number

27. Find the smallest number among
-2, -12, -22.
   a) -22
   b) -2
   c) -12

28. Are -18, -15, 12 in descending order?
   a) False
   b) True

29. Are -9, 5, 7 in ascending order?
   a) True
   b) False

30. Are -15, -14, 13 in descending order?
   a) False
   b) True

31. Write a whole number between
-22 and -20

32. Identify the right relationship to put
numbers in order.
   -15   is the middle number
   -19   is the greatest number
   -18   is the smallest number

33. Are -5, -15, -25 in descending order?
   a) True
   b) False

34. Identify the right relationship to put
numbers in order.
   -4   is the middle number
   -14   is the greatest number
   -9   is the smallest number

35. Are -14, -17, -10 in descending order?
   a) False
   b) True

36. Find the biggest number among
-2, -12, -13.
   a) -2
   b) -12
   c) -13

37. Are -19, -9, -10 in ascending order?
   a) False
   b) True

38. Are 19, 9, -10 in ascending order?
   a) False
   b) True

39. Are -13, -16, -22 in descending order?
   a) True
   b) False

40. Find the smallest number among
-10, -9, -8.
   a) -10
   b) -8
   c) -9

3. NUMBERS REVIEW (TRUE OR FALSE)

1. The square Root of 81 is 9
   a) True
   b) False

2. The least common multiple of 12 and 20 is 60
   a) True
   b) False

3. The square Root of 16 is 4
   a) True
   b) False

4. The square root of 9 is 81
   a) False
   b) True

5. The least common multiple of 3 and 5 is 1
   a) False
   b) True

6. The square of 5 is 25
   a) True
   b) False

7. The square of 3 is 9
   a) True
   b) False

8. The square root of 2 is 4
   a) True
   b) False

9. The square of 25 is 5
   a) False
   b) True

10. The greatest common factor of 6 and 10 is 30
    a) True
    b) False

11. The least common multiple of 15 and 25 is 75
    a) True
    b) False

12. The greatest common factor of 9 and 15 is 3
    a) True
    b) False

13. The greatest common factor of 18 and 30 is 90
    False
    True

14. The square root of 4 is 16
    a) False
    b) True

15. The least common multiple of 9 and 15 is 3
    a) False
    b) True

16. The greatest common factor of 30 and 50 is 10
    a) True
    b) False

17. The square of 2 is 4
    a) False
    b) True

18. The square of 4 is 2
    a) False
    b) True

19. The square of 81 is 9
    a) False
    b) True

20. The square of 16 is 4
    a) False
    b) True

21. The least common multiple of 12 and 20 is 4
    a) False
    b) True

22. The least common multiple of 6 and 10 is 30
    a) False
    b) True

23. The greatest common factor of 21 and 35 is 7
    a) True
    b) False

24. The square of 6 is 36
    a) True
    b) False

25. The least common multiple of 30 and 50 is 150
    a) True
    b) False

26. The square Root of 64 is 8
    a) True
    b) False

27. The greatest common factor of 27 and 45 is 135
    a) False
    b) True

28. The square root of 10 is 100
    a) False
    b) True

29. The least common multiple of

36. The least common multiple of

21 and 35 is 105
  a) True
  b) False

6 and 10 is 2
  a) False
  b) True

30. The square root of 7 is 49
  a) False
  b) True

37. The greatest common factor of 24 and 40 is 120
  a) False
  b) True

31. The square Root of 4 is 2
  a) True
  b) False

38. The greatest common factor of 24 and 40 is 8
  a) True
  b) False

32. The greatest common factor of 9 and 15 is 45
  a) False
  b) True

39. The square of 49 is 7
  a) False
  b) True

33. The square of 36 is 6
  a) False
  b) True

40. The greatest common factor of 18 and 30 is 6
  a) True
  b) False

34. The square of 9 is 81
  a) True
  b) False

35. The square root of 5 is 25
  a) False
  b) True

4. ADDITION AND SUBTRACTION (MISSING NUMBERS)

Solve the following equations and type the missing number:

1. _____ + 135595 = 445150

2. 15835 - _____ = 7864

3. 403965 + _____ = 580582

4. _____ + 83178 = 272098

5. 136470 + _____ = 196858

6. _____ + 105968 = 347338

7. _____ + 108247 = 354862

8. _____ + 126479 = 415054

9. 36815 + _____ = 53902

10. 47305 + _____ = 68950

11. 26325 + _____ = 38854

12. 94510 + _____ = 136666

13. 131225 + _____ = 189334

14. _____ + 90015 = 294670

15. 89265 + _____ = 129142

16. _____ + 131037 = 430102

17. 146960 + _____ = 211906

18. _____ + 103689 = 339814

19. 57795 - _____ = 31592

20. 78775 + _____ = 114094

21. 183675 + _____ = 264574

22. 63040 - _____ = 34558

23. _____ + 85457 = 279622

24. _____ + 158385 = 520390

25. _____ + 133316 = 437626

26. 152205 + _____ = 219430

27. _____ + 153827 = 505342

28. 398720 + _____ = 573058

29. _____ + 149269 = 490294

30. 21080 - _____ = 10830

31. _____ + 87736 = 287146

32. 10590 - _____ = 4898

33. 31570 + _____ = 46378

34. 84020 + _____ = 121618

35. 409210 + _____ = 588106

36. 141715 + _____ = 204382

37. _____ + 128758 = 422578

38. 52550 - _____ = 28626

39. 393475 + _____ = 565534

40. 42060 + _____ = 61426

5. ADDITION AND SUBTRACTION (WORD PROBLEMS)

1.   Joseph collects 4 candies. Joseph's father gives him 8 more candies. How many candies does Joseph have?

2.   Susan has 58 candies. Sandra has 5 candies. If Sandra gives all of her candies to Susan, how many candies will Susan have?

3.   Kim has 80 Skittles. Thomas has 2 Skittles. If Thomas gives all of his Skittles to Kim, how many Skittles will Kim have?

4.   If there are 4 crayons in a box and Beverly puts 4 more crayons inside, how many crayons are in the box?

5.   There are 68 blocks in a box. Chris takes 19 blocks. How many are left?

6.   Tom has 80 cards. He gets 7 more from Jane. How many cards does Tom have in all?

7.   Joseph collects 4 candies. Joseph's father gives Joseph 18 more. How many candies does Joseph have?

8.   Angela has 51 erasers. She gets 5 more from Donna. How many erasers does Angela have in all?

9.   Mary removes 7 candies from a jar. There were originally 36 candies in the jar. How many candies are left in the jar?

10.   Jessica removes 13 bananas from a jar. There were originally 20 bananas in the jar. How many bananas are left in the jar?

11. Tom has 9 candies. Lisa has 4 candies. If Lisa gives all of her candies to Tom, how many candies will Tom have?

12. Kim has 84 Skittles. Thomas has 2 Skittles. If Thomas gives all of his Skittles to Kim, how many Skittles will Kim have?

13. Tim starts with 40 nuts. He gets 5 more from Gregory. How many nuts does Tim end with?

14. Ruth collects 72 crayons. Ruth's father gives Ruth 7 more. How many crayons does Ruth have?

15. There are 68 blocks in a box. Chris takes 18 blocks. How many are left?

16. Tim starts with 35 nuts. He gets 10 more from Gregory. How many nuts does Tim end with?

17. Mary removes 7 candies from a jar. There were originally 33 candies in the jar. How many candies are left in the jar?

18. Linda starts with 93 crayons. She gives 33 to Billy. How many crayons does Linda end with?

19. Angela has 51 erasers. She gets 5 more from Donna. How many erasers does Angela have in all?

20. Tom has 82 cards. He gets 7 more from Jane. How many cards does Tom have in all?

21. Linda starts with 93 crayons. She gives 39 to Billy. How many crayons does Linda end with?

22. Susan has 58 candies. Sandra has 5 candies. If Sandra gives all of her candies to Susan, how many candies will Susan have?

6. ROUNDING AND ESTIMATE NUMBERS

Solve the following equations by rounding off to nearest ten:

1. $62 + 41 + 36 = $ _____

2. $112 + 66 + 56 = $ _____

3. $142 + 81 + 68 = $ _____

4. $202 + 111 + 92 = $ _____

5. $192 + 106 + 88 = $ _____

6. $22 + 21 + 20 = $ _____

7. $132 + 76 + 64 = $ _____

8. $82 + 51 + 44 = $ _____

9. $122 + 71 + 60 = $ _____

10. $212 + 116 + 96 = $ _____

11. $182 + 101 + 84 = $ _____

12. $162 + 91 + 76 = $ _____

13. $32 + 26 + 24 = $ _____

14. $52 + 36 + 32 = $ _____

15. $222 + 121 + 100 = $ _____

16. $102 + 61 + 52 = $ _____

17. $12 + 16 + 16 = $ _____

18. $92 + 56 + 48 = $ _____

19. $42 + 31 + 28 = $ _____

20. $152 + 86 + 72 = $ _____

21. $72 + 46 + 40 = $ _____

22. $172 + 96 + 80 = $ _____

7. ADDITION AND SUBTRACTION FACTS USING DECIMAL NUMBERS

Solve the following addition equations:

1. $236125.55 + 103690.05 =$ _____

2. $241370.56 + 105969.07 =$ _____

3. $288575.65 + 126480.25 =$ _____

4. $42060.18 + 19366.31 =$ _____

5. $146960.38 + 64946.71 =$ _____

6. $99755.29 + 44435.53 =$ _____

7. $26325.15 + 12529.25 =$ _____

8. $299065.67 + 131038.29 =$ _____

9. $141715.37 + 62667.69 =$ _____

10. $152205.39 + 67225.73 =$ _____

11. $257105.59 + 112806.13 =$ _____

12. $136470.36 + 60388.67 =$ _____

13. $188920.46 + 83178.87 =$ _____

14. $84020.26 + 37598.47 =$ _____

15. $31570.16 + 14808.27 =$ _____

16. $78775.25 + 35319.45 =$ _____

17. $94510.28 + 42156.51 =$ _____

18. $183675.45 + 80899.85 =$ _____

19. $246615.57 + 108248.09 =$ _____

20. $293820.66 + 128759.27 =$ _____

21. 199410.48 + 87736.91 = _____

22. 36815.17 + 17087.29 = _____

23. 47305.19 + 21645.33 = _____

24. 131225.35 + 58109.65 = _____

25. 194165.47 + 85457.89 = _____

26. 89265.27 + 39877.49 = _____

27. 204655.49 + 90015.93 = _____

28. 251860.58 + 110527.11 = _____

8. ADD AND SUBTRACT DECIMAL NUMBERS (MISSING NUMBERS)

Type the missing number in the following equations:

1. 84068.43 + _____ = 123267.02

2. 131300.61 + _____ = 191910.47

3. 26340.21 + _____ = 39369.47

4. 141796.65 + _____ = 207164.57

5. 36836.25 + _____ = 54623.57

6. 47332.29 + _____ = 69877.67

7. 94564.47 + _____ = 138521.12

8. 136548.63 + _____ = 199537.52

9. 152292.69 + _____ = 222418.67

10. 147044.67 + _____ = 214791.62

11. 31588.23 + _____ = 46996.52

12. 89316.45 + _____ = 130894.07

13. 78820.41 + _____ = 115639.97

14. 42084.27 + _____ = 62250.62

15. 183780.81 + _____ = 268180.97

16. _____ + 86779.19 = 275808.02

17. 99812.49 + _____ = 146148.17

9. ADD AND SUBTRACT DECIMAL NUMBERS (WORD PROBLEMS)

1.   Aid did Math for 0.46 hours, spent 0.89 hrs. on writing and 0.54 hours on reading on Sunday. How much did he study on Sunday?

2.   John takes 0.33 minutes to solve 1 puzzle, 0.5 minutes to solve second puzzle and 0.66 for another puzzle. How long did he take to solve the 3 puzzles?

3.   John had a balance of 0.47 million dollars in his account and he deposited .92 million more into his account. Then then he withdrew 0.53 million dollars from bank to buy home. What will be the balance in his bank account now?

4.   Josh played for 0.46 hours on computer, 0.88 hrs. on game box and then played outside for 0.54 hours. How much did he play?

5.   Joseph studied for 0.47 hrs. on Sunday morning, 0.90 hrs. on Sunday evening and then studied 0.53 hours on Saturday. How much did she study over weekend?

6.   Matt took .44 hours to clean up the room and then played for .81 hours and .56 hrs. for arranging clothes. How much did he spent on cleanup and playing?

7.   Jeff played on computer for .40 hours and then played on game box for .70 hours and on computer for 0.60 hrs. again. How long did he play?

8.   Susan played for 0.46 hours on Sunday morning, 0.88 hrs. on Sunday evening and played for 0.54 hours on Saturday. How much did he play over the weekend?

9.   Sam played on computer for 0.47 hrs. and game box for .91 hrs. and Usha played for .53 hours overall. How much more did Sam play compare to Usha?

10. Raman played for 0.45 hrs. and then studied for 0.85 hours and then played for 0.55 hrs. How much time did he spend on playing and studying together?

11. Rachel played on game box for 0.48 hrs. and then 0.94 hrs. on computer and studied for only 0.52 hrs. on Sunday. How much extra did Rachel play on Sunday as compared to studies?

12. Joseph spent 0.44 hrs. cleaning and 0.83 hours playing and then 0.56 hrs. on computer. How much time did she spend cleaning and playing?

13. Alisha walks .38 miles to school and then walks .63 miles from school to playground and .63 miles back to home. How much did she walks?

14. John spent $ 0.48 to buy an eraser and $0.93 to buy a pencil. He also returned a sharpener for $0.53. How much money (balance) does he need to pay to the shop keeper now?

15. Samuel played computer for 0.48 hours, game box for 0.93 hrs. and then studied for 0.52 hours. How much extra did Samuel play as compared to studies?

10.   COMPARE AND BALANCE EQUATIONS USING DECIMAL NUMBERS

Compare and balance the following equations by placing comparison sign > or = or <:

1. 1645.26 - 1077.43 ___ 1645.26 - 1073.43

2. 218.09 + 815.22 ___ 815.22 + 218.09

3. 121.11 - 39.24 ___ 81.87

4. 1707.84 - 1187.87 ___ 1707.84 - 1188.87

5. 100.11 + 103.12 ___ 204.23

6. 747.7 + 161.4 ___ 910.1

7. 806.3 + 262.5 ___ 1068.8

8. 1189.39 - 904.78 ___ 1189.39 - 904.78

9. 335.31 + 227.7 ___ 335.31 + 226.7

11. 555.72 + 204.2 ___ 759.92

12. 422.49 + 899.26 ___ 899.26 + 422.49

13. 100.12 + 98.2 ___ 198.32

14. 525.2 - 367.99 ___ 159.21

15. 330.51 + 710.17 ___ 710.17 + 330.51

16. 484.55 - 174.76 ___ 309.79

17. 312.81 + 125.58 ___ 437.39

18. 122.9 + 103.5 ___ 226.4

19. 228.31 + 836.23 ___ 836.23 + 228.31

10. 517.91 + 140.72 ___ 659.63

20. 1426.16 - 936.33 ___ 1426.16 - 934.33

21. 1136.12 - 889.23 ___ 1136.12 - 889.23

31. 1667.6 - 1145.84 ___ 519.76

22. 406.22 - 228.58 ___ 179.64

32. 578.5 + 209.5 ___ 788

23. 783.52 + 257.2 ___ 1040.72

33. 225.21 + 207.4 ___ 225.21 + 206.4

24. 523.51 + 144.98 ___ 667.49

34. 1668.82 - 1044.73 ___ 1668.82 -1044.7?

25. 432.70 + 920.27 ___ 920.27 + 432.70

35. 121 + 105 ___ 227

26. 755.28 + 166.32 ___ 920.6

36. 539.42 - 383.48 ___ 156.94

27. 1722.09 - 1060.28 ___ 1722.09 - 1060.28

37. 320.29 + 689.16 ___ 689.16 + 320.29

28. 102.11 + 106.18 ___ 207.29

38. 726.81 + 159.52 ___ 887.33

29. 1404.15 - 922.22 ___ 1404.15 - 921.22

39. 123.18 + 108.12 ___ 230.3

30. 225.51 + 122.04 ___ 225.51 + 123.04

40. 126.11 + 626.13 ___ 626.13 + 126.11

11.   ROUNDING AND ESTIMATE DECIMAL NUMBERS

Round off each number to nearest integer and estimate the following sums:

1.   241.4 + 62.8 + 48.6 = _____

2.   181.1 + 47.2 + 36.6 = _____

3.   60.5 + 16 + 12.6 = _____

4.   80.6 + 21.2 + 16.6 = _____

5.   100.7 + 26.4 + 20.6 = _____

6.   382.1 + 99.2 - 76.6 = _____

7.   20.3 + 5.6 + 4.6 = _____

8.   221.3 + 57.6 + 44.6 = _____

9.   442.4 + 114.8 - 88.6 = _____

10.   0.2 + 0.4 + 0.6 = _____

11.   301.7 + 78.4 - 60.6 = _____

12.   140.9 + 36.8 + 28.6 = _____

13.   422.3 + 109.6 - 84.6 = _____

14.   321.8 + 83.6 - 64.6 = _____

15.   341.9 + 88.8 - 68.6 = _____

16.   261.5 + 68 + 52.6 = _____

17.   161 + 42 + 32.6 = _____

18.   120.8 + 31.6 + 24.6 = _____

19.   201.2 + 52.4 + 40.6 = _____

20.   362 + 94 - 72.6 = _____

21.   281.6 + 73.2 - 56.6 = _____

22.   402.2 + 104.4 - 80.6 = _____

12.   MULTIPLY BY 1 DIGIT NUMBERS

Multiply the following numbers:

1. 38 x 5 = _____

2. 32 x 6 = _____

3. 25 x 8 = _____

4. 21 x 3 = _____

5. 58 x 5 = _____

6. 27 x 7 = _____

7. 28 x 2 = _____

8. 68 x 5 = _____

9. 63 x 5 = _____

10. 39 x 4 = _____

11. 51 x 4 = _____

12. 25 x 6 = _____

13. 27 x 4 = _____

14. 29 x 7 = _____

15. 39 x 6 = _____

16. 17 x 7 = _____

17. 28 x 8 = _____

18. 48 x 4 = _____

19. 25 x 7 = _____

20. 33 x 5 = _____

21. 36 x 4 = _____   31. 45 x 3 = _____

22. 53 x 5 = _____   32. 24 x 3 = _____

23. 73 x 5 = _____   33. 43 x 5 = _____

24. 48 x 2 = _____   34. 19 x 7 = _____

25. 53 x 6 = _____   35. 34 x 8 = _____

26. 68 x 2 = _____   36. 19 x 8 = _____

27. 42 x 4 = _____   37. 37 x 8 = _____

28. 31 x 7 = _____   38. 15 x 7 = _____

29. 67 x 6 = _____   39. 88 x 6 = _____

30. 27 x 3 = _____   40. 31 x 8 = _____

13.   MULTIPLY BY 2 DIGIT NUMBERS

Multiply the following numbers:

1. 32 x 73 = _____

2. 58 x 65 = _____

3. 21 x 46 = _____

4. 20 x 13 = _____

5. 53 x 30 = _____

6. 38 x 61 = _____

7. 21 x 37 = _____

8. 63 x 66 = _____

9. 32 x 17 = _____

10. 23 x 24 = _____

11. 36 x 51 = _____

12. 54 x 57 = _____

13. 13 x 22 = _____

14. 39 x 52 = _____

15. 18 x 36 = _____

16. 30 x 49 = _____

17. 44 x 21 = _____

18. 33 x 41 = _____

19. 25 x 72 = _____

20. 58 x 31 = _____

21. 68 x 33 = _____

22. 30 x 40 = _____

23. 24 x 47 = _____

24. 48 x 55 = _____

25. 18 x 71 = _____

26. 23 x 58 = _____

27. 26 x 15 = _____

28. 41 x 20 = _____

29. 14 x 11 = _____

30. 12 x 34 = _____

31. 45 x 45 = _____

32. 78 x 69 = _____

33. 11 x 10 = _____

34. 36 x 42 = _____

35. 45 x 54 = _____

36. 33 x 60 = _____

37. 23 x 14 = _____

38. 35 x 18 = _____

39. 43 x 62 = _____

40. 17 x 12 = _____

14. MULTIPLEY 10S, 100S AND 1000S BY 1 DIGIT NUMBERS

Multiply the following numbers:

1. 30 x 8 = _____

2. 10 x 3 = _____

3. 30 x 2 = _____

4. 1400 x 4 = _____

5. 50 x 4 = _____

6. 1600 x 4 = _____

7. 24000 x 4 = _____

8. 70 x 2 = _____

9. 120 x 2 = _____

10. 20 x 5 = _____

11. 50 x 7 = _____

12. 24000 x 6 = _____

13. 1500 x 2 = _____

14. 70 x 6 = _____

15. 50 x 5 = _____

16. 70 x 4 = _____

17. 400 x 3 = _____

18. 16000 x 2 = _____

19. 15000 x 3 = _____

20. 14000 x 6 = _____

21. 12000 x 5 = _____   31. 13000 x 7 = _____

22. 14000 x 2 = _____   32. 20 x 7 = _____

23. 30 x 4 = _____   33. 10 x 5 = _____

24. 200 x 7 = _____   34. 120 x 4 = _____

25. 200 x 5 = _____   35. 30 x 7 = _____

26. 1200 x 2 = _____   36. 1000 x 3 = _____

27. 13000 x 3 = _____   37. 40 x 3 = _____

28. 13000 x 5 = _____   38. 110 x 4 = _____

29. 1400 x 6 = _____   39. 1500 x 4 = _____

30. 14000 x 4 = _____   40. 1600 x 6 = _____

15.   MULTIPLEY 10S, 100S AND 1000S BY 2 DIGIT NUMBERS

Multiply the following numbers:

1. 900 x 11 = _____

2. 90 x 11 = _____

3. 12000 x 11 = _____

4. 40 x 12 = _____

5. 10 x 11 = _____

6. 1000 x 11 = _____

7. 45000 x 11 = _____

8. 700 x 11 = _____

9. 70 x 11 = _____

10. 500 x 11 = _____

11. 30 x 11 = _____

12. 50 x 11 = _____

13. 20 x 12 = _____

14. 23000 x 11 = _____

16.   PROPERTIES OF MULTIPLICATION

1. Identify and match the right multiplication property.
     Associative Property   7 x 1 = 7
     Commutative Property   7 x (10 x 16) = (7 x 10) x 16
     Identity Property   7 x (10 x 16) = (10 x 16) x 7

2. Which of the following equations represents identity property of multiplication?
     a) 8 x 1 = 8
     b) 8 x (11 x 18) = (8 x 11) x 18
     c) 8 x (11 x 18) = (11 x 18) x 8

3. Which of the following equations represents identity property of multiplication?
     a) 12 x 1 = 12
     b) 12 x (15 x 26) = (12 x 15) x 26
     c) 12 x (15 x 26) = (15 x 26) x 12

4. Identify and match the right multiplication property.
     Associative Property   11 x 1 = 11
     Commutative Property   11 x (9 x 13) = (11 x 9) x 13
     Identity Property   11 x (9 x 13) = (9 x 13) x 11

5. Which of the following equations represents identity property of multiplication?
     a) 9 x 1 = 9
     b) 9 x (12 x 20) = (9 x 12) x 20
     c) 9 x (12 x 20) = (12 x 20) x 9

6. Which of the following equations represents associative property of multiplication?
     a) 9 x 1 = 9
     b) 9 x (12 x 13) = (9 x 12) x 13
     c) 9 x (12 x 13) = (12 x 13) x 9

7. Which of the following equations represents commutative property of multiplication?
    a) $9 \times 1 = 9$
    b) $9 \times (12 \times 13) = (9 \times 12) \times 13$
    c) $9 \times (12 \times 13) = (12 \times 13) \times 9$

8. Which of the following equations represents commutative property of multiplication?
    a) $11 \times 1 = 11$
    b) $11 \times (14 \times 24) = (11 \times 14) \times 24$
    c) $11 \times (14 \times 24) = (14 \times 24) \times 11$

9. Which of the following equations represents commutative property of multiplication?
    a) $12 \times 1 = 12$
    b) $12 \times (15 \times 26) = (12 \times 15) \times 26$
    c) $12 \times (15 \times 26) = (15 \times 26) \times 12$

10. Identify and match the right multiplication property.
Associative Property	$5 \times 1 = 5$
Commutative Property	$5 \times (7 \times 11) = (5 \times 7) \times 11$
Identity Property	$5 \times (7 \times 11) = (7 \times 11) \times 5$

11. Identify and match the right multiplication property.
Associative Property	$14 \times 1 = 14$
Commutative Property	$14 \times (10 \times 14) = (14 \times 10) \times 14$
Identity Property	$14 \times (10 \times 14) = (10 \times 14) \times 14$

12. Identify and match the right multiplication property.
Associative Property	$5 \times 1 = 5$
Commutative Property	$5 \times (8 \times 12) = (5 \times 8) \times 12$
Identity Property	$5 \times (8 \times 12) = (8 \times 12) \times 5$

13. Identify and match the right multiplication property.
      Associative Property   8 x 1 = 8
      Commutative Property   8 x (8 x 12) = (8 x 8) x 12
      Identity Property   8 x (8 x 12) = (8 x 12) x 8

14. Which of the following equations represents identity property of multiplication?
    a) 10 x 1 = 10
    b) 10 x (13 x 22) = (10 x 13) x 22
    c) 10 x (13 x 22) = (13 x 22) x 10

15. Identify and match the right multiplication property.
      Associative Property   2 x 1 = 2
      Commutative Property   2 x (6 x 10) = (2 x 6) x 10
      Identity Property   2 x (6 x 10) = (6 x 10) x 2

16. Identify and match the right multiplication property.
      Associative Property   6 x 1 = 6
      Commutative Property   6 x (9 x 14) = (6 x 9) x 14
      Identity Property   6 x (9 x 14) = (9 x 14) x 6

17. Which of the following equations represents identity property of multiplication?
    a) 11 x 1 = 11
    b) 11 x (14 x 24) = (11 x 14) x 24
    c) 11 x (14 x 24) = (14 x 24) x 11

18. Identify and match the right multiplication property.
      Associative Property   4 x 1 = 4
      Commutative Property   4 x (7 x 10) = (4 x 7) x 10
      Identity Property   4 x (7 x 10) = (7 x 10) x 4

19. Which of the following equations represents commutative property of multiplication?
    a) 11 x 1 = 11
    b) 11 x (15 x 18) = (11 x 15) x 18
    c) 11 x (15 x 18) = (15 x 18) x 11

20. Which of the following equations represents associative property of multiplication?
    a) 13 x 1 = 13
    b) 13 x (18 x 23) = (13 x 18) x 23
    c) 13 x (18 x 23) = (18 x 23) x 13

21. Identify and match the right multiplication property.
    Associative Property   3 x 1 = 3
    Commutative Property   3 x (6 x 8) = (3 x 6) x 8
    Identity Property   3 x (6 x 8) = (6 x 8) x 3

22. Which of the following equations represents associative property of multiplication?
    a) 11 x 1 = 11
    b) 11 x (15 x 18) = (11 x 15) x 18
    c) 11 x (15 x 18) = (15 x 18) x 11

23. Which of the following equations represents associative property of multiplication?
    a) 15 x 1 = 15
    b) 15 x (21 x 28) = (15 x 21) x 28
    c) 15 x (21 x 28) = (21 x 28) x 15

24. Which of the following equations represents commutative property of multiplication?
    a) 13 x 1 = 13
    b) 13 x (18 x 23) = (13 x 18) x 23
    c) 13 x (18 x 23) = (18 x 23) x 13

25. Which of the following equations represents associative property of multiplication?
    a) 17 x 1 = 17
    b) 17 x (24 x 33) = (17 x 24) x 33
    c) 17 x (24 x 33) = (24 x 33) x 17

17.   MULTIPLICATION AND DISTRIBUTIVE PROPERTIES

Type the missing factor in the following equations:

1. 7 x (14 x 10) = (7 x _____) x 10

2. 9 x (_____ + 12) = 9 x 18 + 9 x 12

3. 6 x (12 + 9) = 6 x 12 + _____ x 9

4. _____ x (4 + 5) = 2 x 4 + 2 x 5

5. 6 x (12 + _____) = 6 x 12 + 6 x 9

6. 2 x (4 x 5) = (_____ x 5) x 4

7. 10 x (_____ + 13) = 10 x 20 + 10 x 13

8. 7 x (14 + _____) = 7 x 14 + 7 x 10

9. 2 x 3 = 3 x _____

10. 3 x (6 x 6) = (3 x 6) x _____

11. 7 x (14 x _____) = (7 x 10) x 14

12. 8 x (16 + 11) = 8 x 16 + _____ x 11

13. 3 x 6 = 6 x _____

14. 8 x 21 = _____ x 8

15. 1 x (2 + 4) = 1 x 2 + 1 x _____

16. 10 x (20 x _____) = (10 x 13) x 20

17. 8 x (16 x _____) = (8 x 11) x 16

18. 7 x (14 + 10) = 7 x 14 + _____ x 10

19. 8 x (16 + _____) = 8 x 16 + 8 x 11

20. 9 x (18 + 12) = 9 x 18 + _____ x 12

21. _____ x (6 + 6) = 3 x 6 + 3 x 6

22. _____ x (8 + 7) = 4 x 8 + 4 x 7

23. 4 x (8 x 7) = (_____ x 7) x 8

24. 6 x (12 x 9) = (6 x _____) x 9

25. 1 x (2 x 4) = (_____ x 4) x 2

26. 29 x 27 = _____ x 29

27. 4 x (8 + 7) = 4 x 8 + 4 x _____

28. 9 x 24 = _____ x 9

29. _____ x (2 + 4) = 1 x 2 + 1 x 4

30. 7 x 18 = _____ x 7

31. 1 x (2 x 4) = (1 x 2) x _____

32. 10 x (20 + _____) = 10 x 20 + 10 x 13

33. 5 x (10 x 8) = (5 x 10) x _____

34. _____ x (10 + 8) = 5 x 10 + 5 x 8

35. 4 x (8 x 7) = (4 x 8) x _____

36. 2 x (4 + 5) = 2 x 4 + 2 x _____

37. 6 x (_____ + 9) = 6 x 12 + 6 x 9

38. 5 x (10 + 8) = 5 x 10 + 5 x _____

39. 9 x (18 + _____) = 9 x 18 + 9 x 12

40. 5 x (10 x 8) = (_____ x 8) x 10

18. ROUNDING AND MULTIPLICATION

Round off each factor (number) to nearest ten and then multiply:

1. 93 x 62 = _____

2. 27 x 79 = _____

3. 52 x 21 = _____

4. 21 x 74 = _____

5. 36 x 88 = _____

6. 53 x 22 = _____

7. 29 x 87 = _____

8. 94 x 63 = _____

9. 51 x 14 = _____

10. 19 x 77 = _____

11. 31 x 84 = _____

12. 64 x 33 = _____

13. 72 x 41 = _____

14. 33 x 92 = _____

15. 44 x 13 = _____

16. 43 x 12 = _____

17. 28 x 86 = _____

18. 92 x 61 = _____

19. 14 x 73 = _____

20. 62 x 31 = _____

21. 16 x 68 = _____

22. 74 x 43 = _____

23. 11 x 64 = _____

24. 23 x 82 = _____

25. 71 x 34 = _____

26. 13 x 72 = _____

27. 83 x 52 = _____

28. 26 x 78 = _____

29. 61 x 24 = _____

30. 41 x 94 = _____

31. 91 x 54 = _____

32. 12 x 71 = _____

33. 82 x 51 = _____

34. 24 x 83 = _____

35. 17 x 69 = _____

36. 22 x 81 = _____

37. 81 x 44 = _____

38. 37 x 89 = _____

39. 63 x 32 = _____

40. 34 x 93 = _____

19.   MULTIPLY BY 1 AND 2 DIGIT NUMBERS (MISSING FACTOR)

Type the missing factor in the following equations:

1. 22 x _____ = 330

2. 24 x _____ = 384

3. 34 x _____ = 544

4. 57 x _____ = 627

5. 21 x _____ = 315

6. 36 x _____ = 108

7. 93 x _____ = 1302

8. 69 x _____ = 345

9. 24 x _____ = 48

10. 47 x _____ = 188

11. 70 x _____ = 840

12. 71 x _____ = 923

13. 69 x _____ = 828

14. 48 x _____ = 528

15. 81 x _____ = 486

16. 60 x _____ = 720

17. 45 x _____ = 765

18. 47 x _____ = 517

19. 35 x _____ = 105

20. 33 x _____ = 66

21. 70 x _____ = 350

22. 35 x _____ = 350

23. 45 x _____ = 450

24. 34 x _____ = 68

25. 59 x _____ = 708

26. 72 x _____ = 432

27. 33 x _____ = 528

28. 22 x _____ = 176

29. 83 x _____ = 581

30. 23 x _____ = 368

31. 36 x _____ = 612

32. 12 x _____ = 96

33. 24 x _____ = 216

34. 81 x _____ = 1053

35. 21 x _____ = 168

36. 82 x _____ = 1066

37. 84 x _____ = 1176

38. 48 x _____ = 864

39. 46 x _____ = 782

40. 46 x _____ = 138

20.   MULTIPLY BY 1 AND 2 DIGIT NUMBERS (TRUE OR FALSE)

Verify each of the following multiplication whether it is correct (true) or not (false):

1. True or False: 27 x 12 = 324
    a) True
    b) False

8. True or False: 14 x 11 = 154
    a) True
    b) False

2. True or False: 23 x 7 = 161
    a) True
    b) False

9. True or False: 23 x 16 = 368
    a) True
    b) False

3. True or False: 12 x 11 = 132
    a) True
    b) False

10. True or False: 43 x 8 = 344
    a) True
    b) False

4. True or False: 17 x 11 = 187
    a) True
    b) False

11. True or False: 35 x 17 = 595
    a) True
    b) False

5. True or False: 24 x 7 = 168
    True
    False

12. True or False: 24 x 12 = 288
    a) True
    b) False

6. True or False: 25 x 12 = 300
    True
    False

13. True or False: 51 x 5 = 255
    a) True
    b) False

7. True or False: 16 x 15 = 240
    True
    False

14. True or False: 18 x 2 = 37
    a) False
    b) True

15. True or False: 15 x 6 = 90
    a) True
    b) False

23. True or False: 26 x 12 = 312
    a) True
    b) False

16. True or False: 33 x 12 = 396
    a) True
    b) False

24. True or False: 26 x 7 = 182
    a) True
    b) False

17. True or False: 25 x 7 = 175
    a) True
    b) False

25. True or False: 42 x 8 = 336
    a) True
    b) False

18. True or False: 37 x 13 = 481
    a) True
    b) False

26. True or False: 15 x 15 = 225
    a) True
    b) False

19. True or False: 14 x 15 = 210
    a) True
    b) False

27. True or False: 35 x 13 = 455
    a) True
    b) False

20. True or False: 46 x 18 = 828
    a) True
    b) False

28. True or False: 24 x 16 = 384
    a) True
    b) False

21. True or False: 45 x 14 = 630
    a) True
    b) False

29. True or False: 37 x 17 = 629
    a) True
    b) False

22. True or False: 14 x 6 = 84
    a) True
    b) False

30. True or False: 47 x 14 = 658
    a) True
    b) False

31. True or False: 12 x 15 = 180

36. True or False: 54 x 14 = 756

a) True
b) False

a) True
b) False

32. True or False: 26 x 16 = 416
   a) True
   b) False

37. True or False: 47 x 18 = 846
   a) True
   b) False

33. True or False: 23 x 12 = 276
   a) True
   b) False

38. True or False: 13 x 15 = 195
   a) True
   b) False

34. True or False: 32 x 7 = 224
   a) True
   b) False

39. True or False: 46 x 14 = 644
   a) True
   b) False

35. True or False: 46 x 9 = 414
   a) True
   b) False

40. True or False: 36 x 13 = 468
   a) True
   b) False

21.   MULTIPLY BY 1 AND 2 DIGIT NUMBERS (WORD PROBLEMS)

1.   A large box has toys worth $242 and a small box has toys worth $60. What is the total dollar value of toys in 5 small and 2 large boxes?

2.   A man in Africa walks 10 miles for work and then comes back the same distance back home. How much distance will he travel in 44 days?

3.   A Tiger eats $25 worth of meat daily. How much will he eat in 4 weeks (28 days)?

4.   Each student contributed $5 for the trip. If there were 28 kids in all, how much money was collected?

5.   A lion eats $12 worth of meat daily. How much will he eat in 30 days?

6.   A chef cooked $50 worth of chicken daily in the restaurant. How much will he cook in 2 weeks (14 days)?

7.   A chef sells $24 worth of soup daily. How much will he sell in 15 days?

8.   Lisa collected $10 during fall sale day. The sale is for 13 days. Assuming each day, she collects the same amount, how much will she collect in 13 days?

9.   Each kid donated $3 for flood relief. If there are 247 kids who donated. How much money was collected?

10.   If you will deposit $23 every week for the next 5 years. How much money will you have by end of 5th year.

22. IDENTIFY MULTIPLICAND, MULTIPLIER AND PRODUCTS

1. What is multiplier in the equation: 15 x 21 = 315?
   a) 15
   b) 21
   c) 315

2. What is the product value in the equation: 9 x 12 = 108?
   a) 9
   b) 12
   c) 108

3. Identify multiplicand, multiplier and products in the equation 6 x 9 = 54
   Multiplier   6
   Product   9
   Multiplicand   54

4. What is multiplier in the equation: 17 x 24 = 408?
   a) 17
   b) 24
   c) 408

5. What is the value of multiplicand in the equation: 11 x 14 = 154?
   a) 11
   b) 14
   c) 154

6. What is the value of multiplicand in the equation: 12 x 15 = 180?
   a) 12
   b) 15
   c) 180

7. Identify multiplicand, multiplier and products in the equation 2 x 6 = 12
   Multiplier   2
   Product   6
   Multiplicand   12

8. Identify multiplicand, multiplier and products in the equation 8 x 8 = 64
   Multiplier   8
   Product   8
   Multiplicand   64

9. What is multiplier in the equation: 9 x 12 = 108?
   a) 9
   b) 12
   c) 108

10. Identify multiplicand, multiplier and products in the equation 4 x 7 = 28
   Multiplier   4
   Product   7
   Multiplicand   28

11. What is multiplier in the equation: 13 x 18 = 234?
   a) 13
   b) 18
   c) 234

12. What is the product value in the equation: 11 x 15 = 165?
   a) 11
   b) 15
   c) 165

13. What is multiplier in the equation: 11 x 15 = 165?
   a) 11
   b) 15
   c) 165

14. What is the value of multiplicand in the equation: 9 x 12 = 108?
   a) 9
   b) 12
   c) 108

15. Identify multiplicand, multiplier and products in the equation 5 x 8 = 40

Multiplier	5
Product	8
Multiplicand	40

16. What is the value of multiplicand in the equation: 8 x 11 = 88?
   a) 8
   b) 11
   c) 88

17. Identify multiplicand, multiplier and products in the equation 5 x 7 = 35

Multiplier	5
Product	7
Multiplicand	35

18. Identify multiplicand, multiplier and products in the equation 14 x 10 = 140

Multiplier	14
Product	10
Multiplicand	140

19. Identify multiplicand, multiplier and products in the equation 3 x 6 = 18

Multiplier	3
Product	6
Multiplicand	18

20. What is the product value in the equation: 13 x 18 = 234?
   a) 13
   b) 18
   c) 234

21. Identify multiplicand, multiplier and products in the equation 11 x 9 = 99

Multiplier	11
Product	9
Multiplicand	99

22. Identify multiplicand, multiplier and products in the equation 7 x 10 = 70

Multiplier	7
Product	10
Multiplicand	70

23. What is the value of multiplicand in the equation: 10 x 13 = 130?

a) 10
b) 13
c) 130

24. What is the product value in the equation: 11 x 14 = 154?

a) 11
b) 14
c) 154

25. What is the product value in the equation: 12 x 15 = 180?

a) 12
b) 15
c) 180

23.   MULTIPLY 3 DIGIT NUMBER BY 1 DIGIT NUMBER

Multiply the following numbers:

1. 473 x 3 = _____

2. 605 x 4 = _____

3. 449 x 8 = _____

4. 485 x 3 = _____

5. 521 x 3 = _____

6. 509 x 8 = _____

7. 137 x 6 = _____

8. 749 x 5 = _____

9. 665 x 9 = _____

10. 113 x 1 = _____

11. 389 x 3 = _____

12. 473 x 8 = _____

13. 281 x 7 = _____

14. 401 x 3 = _____

15. 593 x 4 = _____

16. 677 x 5 = _____

17. 329 x 2 = _____

18. 101 x 6 = _____

19. 329 x 7 = _____

20. 581 x 9 = _____

21. 221 x 1 = _____

22. 125 x 1 = _____

23. 797 x 5 = _____

24. 521 x 8 = _____

25. 209 x 1 = _____

26. 257 x 2 = _____

27. 185 x 6 = _____

28. 533 x 4 = _____

29. 665 x 4 = _____

30. 221 x 6 = _____

31. 413 x 8 = _____

32. 185 x 1 = _____

33. 281 x 2 = _____

34. 293 x 2 = _____

35. 269 x 7 = _____

36. 125 x 6 = _____

37. 245 x 7 = _____

38. 641 x 9 = _____

39. 761 x 5 = _____

40. 149 x 1 = _____

24.   MULTIPLY 3 DIGIT NUMBER BY 2 DIGIT NUMBER

Multiply the following numbers:

1. 478 x 39 = _____

2. 140 x 49 = _____

3. 205 x 54 = _____

4. 426 x 35 = _____

5. 166 x 51 = _____

6. 504 x 41 = _____

7. 517 x 42 = _____

8. 543 x 44 = _____

9. 218 x 55 = _____

10. 140 x 13 = _____

11. 348 x 29 = _____

12. 244 x 21 = _____

13. 361 x 30 = _____

14. 296 x 61 = _____

15. 270 x 23 = _____

16. 530 x 43 = _____

17. 374 x 67 = _____

18. 335 x 64 = _____

19. 153 x 14 = _____

20. 452 x 37 = _____

21. 166 x 15 = _____   31. 270 x 59 = _____

22. 491 x 40 = _____   32. 335 x 28 = _____

23. 192 x 17 = _____   33. 400 x 33 = _____

24. 400 x 69 = _____   34. 556 x 45 = _____

25. 283 x 24 = _____   35. 374 x 31 = _____

26. 218 x 19 = _____   36. 127 x 48 = _____

27. 413 x 70 = _____   37. 387 x 68 = _____

28. 296 x 25 = _____   38. 101 x 10 = _____

29. 257 x 58 = _____   39. 322 x 63 = _____

30. 244 x 57 = _____   40. 465 x 38 = _____

25.   MULTIPLY 3 DIGIT NUMBER BY 3 DIGIT NUMBER

Multiply the following numbers:

1. 296 x 195 = _____

2. 257 x 234 = _____

3. 218 x 117 = _____

4. 309 x 182 = _____

5. 322 x 169 = _____

6. 205 x 130 = _____

7. 426 x 222 = _____

8. 387 x 104 = _____

9. 179 x 156 = _____

10. 114 x 221 = _____

11. 231 x 104 = _____

12. 205 x 130 = _____

13. 348 x 143 = _____

14. 478 x 170 = _____

15. 309 x 182 = _____

16. 543 x 105 = _____

17. 270 x 221 = _____

18. 452 x 196 = _____

19. 400 x 101 = _____

20. 166 x 169 = _____

21. 348 x 143 = _____   31. 153 x 182 = _____

22. 374 x 117 = _____   32. 140 x 195 = _____

23. 387 x 104 = _____   33. 140 x 195 = _____

24. 504 x 144 = _____   34. 231 x 104 = _____

25. 270 x 221 = _____   35. 218 x 117 = _____

26. 114 x 221 = _____   36. 491 x 157 = _____

27. 283 x 208 = _____   37. 166 x 169 = _____

28. 101 x 234 = _____   38. 335 x 156 = _____

29. 296 x 195 = _____   39. 322 x 169 = _____

30. 127 x 208 = _____   40. 192 x 143 = _____

26.   MULTIPLY 3 WHOLE NUMBERS

Multiply the following numbers:

1. 17 x 9 x 7 = _____

2. 1 x 27 x 2 = _____

3. 5 x 23 x 6 = _____

4. 2 x 24 x 10 = _____

5. 12 x 14 x 2 = _____

6. 1 x 25 x 9 = _____

7. 18 x 8 x 8 = _____

8. 20 x 6 x 10 = _____

9. 10 x 18 x 2 = _____

10. 15 x 13 x 7 = _____

11. 7 x 21 x 8 = _____

12. 3 x 23 x 2 = _____

13. 9 x 19 x 10 = _____

14. 13 x 13 x 3 = _____

15. 17 x 11 x 9 = _____

16. 6 x 20 x 5 = _____

17. 25 x 3 x 8 = _____

18. 10 x 16 x 9 = _____

19. 4 x 22 x 3 = _____

20. 19 x 9 x 2 = _____

21. $2 \times 26 \times 3 =$ _____

22. $6 \times 22 \times 7 =$ _____

23. $20 \times 8 \times 3 =$ _____

24. $11 \times 15 \times 10 =$ _____

25. $16 \times 12 \times 8 =$ _____

26. $8 \times 20 \times 9 =$ _____

27. $24 \times 4 \times 7 =$ _____

28. $21 \times 5 \times 2 =$ _____

29. $12 \times 16 \times 4 =$ _____

30. $14 \times 14 \times 6 =$ _____

31. $8 \times 18 \times 7 =$ _____

32. $19 \times 7 \times 9 =$ _____

33. $14 \times 12 \times 4 =$ _____

34. $25 \times 1 \times 6 =$ _____

35. $4 \times 24 \times 5 =$ _____

36. $7 \times 19 \times 6 =$ _____

37. $23 \times 3 \times 4 =$ _____

38. $24 \times 2 \times 5 =$ _____

39. $11 \times 17 \times 3 =$ _____

40. $13 \times 15 \times 5 =$ _____

27.   MULTIPLY 3 WHOLE NUMBERS (MISSING NUMBERS)

Multiply the following numbers and type the missing number:

1. 5 x _____ x 10 = 500

2. 14 x _____ x 4 = 224

3. 10 x _____ x 9 = 900

4. 7 x _____ x 3 = 42

5. 9 x 2 x _____ = 162

6. 14 x 9 x _____ = 756

7. 6 x _____ x 2 = 12

8. 10 x _____ x 6 = 300

9. 15 x _____ x 5 = 375

10. 15 x 10 x _____ = 1050

11. 1 x _____ x 6 = 36

12. 10 x 5 x _____ = 100

13. 5 x 6 x _____ = 120

14. 6 x 1 x _____ = 42

15. 2 x 9 x _____ = 126

16. 7 x _____ x 6 = 294

17. 1 x _____ x 9 = 9

18. 8 x _____ x 7 = 448

19. 13 x _____ x 3 = 117

20. 7 x 4 x _____ = 56

21. 7 x 2 x _____ = 112

22. 2 x _____ x 10 = 40

23. 9 x 4 x _____ = 360

24. 6 x 5 x _____ = 90

25. 5 x 10 x _____ = 300

26. 9 x _____ x 8 = 648

27. 3 x 8 x _____ = 144

28. 3 x 6 x _____ = 72

29. 8 x _____ x 4 = 96

30. 4 x 7 x _____ = 140

31. 4 x _____ x 9 = 324

32. 11 x 6 x _____ = 198

33. 1 x 10 x _____ = 80

34. 9 x _____ x 5 = 180

35. 12 x 7 x _____ = 336

36. 8 x 3 x _____ = 240

37. 11 x _____ x 10 = 110

38. 13 x 8 x _____ = 520

39. 4 x _____ x 3 = 48

40. 3 x _____ x 8 = 192

28.   MULTIPLY 4 DIGIT NUMBER BY 3 DIGIT NUMBER

Multiply the following numbers:

1.   1576 x 169 = _____

2.   4796 x 118 = _____

3.   5256 x 221 = _____

4.   5026 x 102 = _____

5.   1116 x 221 = _____

6.   1806 x 143 = _____

7.   4451 x 157 = _____

8.   1001 x 234 = _____

9.   3416 x 117 = _____

10.   4566 x 144 = _____

11.   6751 x 208 = _____

12.   2726 x 195 = _____

13.   2496 x 221 = _____

14.   2036 x 117 = _____

15.   4911 x 105 = _____

16.   6866 x 195 = _____

17.   1231 x 208 = _____

18.   1691 x 156 = _____

19.   4681 x 131 = _____

20.   5946 x 143 = _____

21. 3071 x 156 = _____   31. 7096 x 169 = _____

22. 6636 x 221 = _____   32. 4221 x 183 = _____

23. 3531 x 104 = _____   33. 4106 x 196 = _____

24. 7211 x 156 = _____   34. 1346 x 195 = _____

25. 2151 x 104 = _____   35. 5486 x 195 = _____

26. 2956 x 169 = _____   36. 6291 x 104 = _____

27. 2381 x 234 = _____   37. 3301 x 130 = _____

28. 4336 x 170 = _____   38. 3991 x 209 = _____

29. 5716 x 169 = _____   39. 6406 x 101 = _____

30. 2841 x 182 = _____   40. 3186 x 143 = _____

29. MULTIPLICATION PATTERNS

Complete the following multiplication patterns using given hints:

1. If 5 x 9 = 45   Then 5 x 9000 = _____

2. If 2 x 3 = 6   Then 2 x 300 = _____

3. If 5 x 9 = 45   Then 5 x 900 = _____

4. If 10 x 19 = 190   Then 10 x 1900 = _____

5. If 11 x 21 = 231   Then 11 x 210 = _____

6. If 25 x 8 = 200   Then 25 x 8000 = _____

11. If 8 x 15 = 120   Then 8 x 150 = _____

12. If 26 x 7 = 182   Then 26 x 7000 = _____

13. If 3 x 5 = 15   Then 3 x 50 = _____

14. If 3 x 5 = 15   Then 3 x 500 = _____

15. If 10 x 19 = 190   Then 10 x 19000 = _____

16. If 6 x 11 = 66   Then 6 x 1100 = _____

17. If 7 x 13 = 91   Then 7 x 1300 = _____

18. If 17 x 6 = 102   Then 17 x 600 = _____

7. If 16 x 7 = 112   Then 16 x 700 =   19. If 4 x 7 = 28   Then 4 x 7000 = _____

                                                      20. If 6 x 11 = 66   Then 6 x 11000 = _____

_____

8. If 23 x 10 = 230   Then 23 x 10000 =

_____

9. If 27 x 6 = 162   Then 27 x 6000 =

_____

10. If 11 x 21 = 231   Then 11 x 21000 =

_____

21. If 6 x 11 = 66   Then 6 x 110 = _____   31. If 22 x 11 = 242   Then 22 x 11000 =

22. If 8 x 15 = 120   Then 8 x 15000 =   _____

_____

                                                      32. If 2 x 3 = 6   Then 2 x 30 = _____

23. If 7 x 13 = 91   Then 7 x 130 = _____   33. If 11 x 21 = 231   Then 11 x 2100 =

24. If 24 x 9 = 216   Then 24 x 9000 =   _____

34. If 8 x 15 = 120   Then 8 x 1500 = _____

25. If 19 x 4 = 76   Then 19 x 400 =   35. If 3 x 5 = 15   Then 3 x 5000 = _____

_____

36. If 15 x 8 = 120   Then 15 x 800 = _____

26. If 21 x 2 = 42   Then 21 x 200 =   37. If 9 x 17 = 153   Then 9 x 170 = _____

_____

38. If 20 x 3 = 60   Then 20 x 300 = _____

27. If 12 x 11 = 132   Then 12 x 1100 =   39. If 9 x 17 = 153   Then 9 x 17000 =

_____   _____

28. If 10 x 19 = 190   Then 10 x 190 =   40. If 18 x 5 = 90   Then 18 x 500 = _____

_____

29. If 5 x 9 = 45   Then 5 x 90 = _____

30. If 14 x 9 = 126   Then 14 x 900 =

_____

30.   MULTIPLY 10S, 100S, 1000S BY DECIMAL NUMBERS

Multiply the following numbers and calculate the product value up to 2 decimal places:

1. 8000 x 13.5 = _____

2. 400 x 5.67 = _____

3. 10 x 2.5 = _____

4. 80 x 10.23 = _____

5. 20 x 3.6 = _____

6. 500 x 9.34 = _____

7. 1000 x 27.69 = _____

8. 70 x 9.11 = _____

9. 6000 x 46.04 = _____

10. 2000 x 31.36 = _____

11. 60 x 8.32 = _____

12. 3000 x 35.03 = _____

13. 7000 x 12.4 = _____

14. 600 x 13.01 = _____

15. 9000 x 14.6 = _____

16. 40 x 5.8 = _____

17. 10000 x 5.67 = _____

18. 50 x 6.9 = _____

19. 100 x 12.4 = _____

20. 700 x 16.68 = _____

21. 5000 x 42.37 = _____

22. 200 x 13.5 = _____

23. 900 x 24.02 = _____

24. 800 x 20.35 = _____

25. 30 x 4.7 = _____

26. 90 x 11.35 = _____

27. 4000 x 38.72 = _____

28. 300 x 14.6 = _____

31. DECIMAL NUMBERS MULTIPLICATION (TRUE OR FALSE)

Verify each of the following multiplication whether it is correct (true) or not (false):

1. Is 18.25 x 18.86 = 345.195
   a) False
   b) True

2. Is 21.57 x 3.12 = 67.2984
   a) True
   b) False

3. Is 31.02 x 21.57 = 669.1014
   a) True
   b) False

4. Is 28.3 x 23.2 = 659.56
   a) False
   b) True

5. Is 35.22 x 4.57 = 160.9554
   a) True
   b) False

6. Is 30.31 x 29.62 = 900.7822
   a) False
   b) True

7. Is 17.37 x 15.43 = 268.0191
   a) True
   b) False

8. Is 22.27 x 12.63 = 283.2701
   a) False
   b) True

9. Is 18.92 x 20.87 = 396.8604
   a) False
   b) True

10. Is 22.94 x 14.87 = 343.1178
    a) False
    b) True

11. Is 42.57 x 27.81 = 1183.8717
    a) True
    b) False

12. Is 26.96 x 18.92 = 513.0832
    a) False
    b) True

13. Is 14.9 x 8.81 = 132.269
    a) False
    b) True

14. Is 20.93 x 8.15 = 172.5795
    a) False
    b) True

15. Is 19.47 x 20.75 = 404.0025
    a) True
    b) False

16. Is 36.27 x 7.89 = 286.1703
    a) True
    b) False

17. Is 18.42 x 18.09 = 333.2178
    a) True
    b) False

18. Is 25.62 x 23.83 = 613.5246
    a) False
    b) True

19. Is 24.95 x 21.59 = 541.6705
    a) False
    b) True

20. Is 37.32 x 11.21 = 418.3572
    a) True
    b) False

21. Is 32.07 x 23.62 = 757.4934
    a) True
    b) False

22. Is 23.61 x 17.11 = 405.9671
    a) False
    b) True

23. Is 24.28 x 19.35 = 471.818
    a) False
    b) True

24. Is 19.59 x 3.67 = 73.8953
    a) False
    b) True

25. Is 33.12 x 25.67 = 850.1904
    a) True
    b) False

26. Is 20.52 x 23.41 = 480.3732
    a) True
    b) False

27. Is 27.87 x 15.42 = 429.7554
    a) True
    b) False

28. Is 21.6 x 10.39 = 226.424
    a) False
    b) True

29. Is 27.63 x 21.06 = 584.8878
    a) False
    b) True

30. Is 25.77 x 11.32 = 291.7164
    a) True
    b) False

31. Is 34.17 x 27.72 = 947.1924
    a) True
    b) False

36. Is 41.52 x 24.49 = 1016.8248
    a) True
    b) False

32. Is 28.92 x 17.47 = 505.2324
    a) True
    b) False

37. Is 13.56 x 4.79 = 65.9524
    a) False
    b) True

33. Is 14.22 x 7.45 = 105.939
    a) True
    b) False

38. Is 13.17 x 4.79 = 63.0843
    a) True
    b) False

34. Is 24.72 x 9.27 = 229.1544
    a) True
    b) False

39. Is 40.47 x 21.17 = 856.7499
    a) True
    b) False

35. Is 26.82 x 13.37 = 358.5834
    a) True
    b) False

40. Is 23.67 x 7.22 = 170.8974
    a) True
    b) False

32.   MULTIPLY A DECIMAL NUMBER BY 1 DIGIT WHOLE NUMBER

Multiply the following numbers:

1. 63.47 x 3 = _____

2. 12.62 x 6 = _____

3. 44.55 x 7 = _____

4. 11.25 x 2 = _____

5. 39.53 x 5 = _____

6. 22.79 x 6 = _____

7. 41.51 x 4 = _____

8. 51.65 x 2 = _____

9. 55.69 x 5 = _____

10. 47.61 x 2 = _____

11. 32.39 x 4 = _____

12. 17.19 x 4 = _____

13. 32.96 x 6 = _____

14. 15.29 x 2 = _____

15. 12.62 x 3 = _____

16. 93.98 x 6 = _____

17. 63.47 x 6 = _____

18. 23.27 x 7 = _____

19. 73.64 x 3 = _____

20. 14.15 x 4 = _____

21. 23.27 x 4 = _____

22. 31.45 x 5 = _____

23. 29.35 x 7 = _____

24. 53.3 x 3 = _____

25. 43.13 x 6 = _____

26. 53.3 x 6 = _____

27. 39.53 x 2 = _____

28. 11.11 x 4 = _____

29. 32.39 x 7 = _____

30. 31.45 x 2 = _____

31. 15.29 x 5 = _____

32. 73.64 x 3 = _____

33. 26.31 x 4 = _____

34. 38.47 x 7 = _____

35. 93.98 x 3 = _____

36. 35.43 x 4 = _____

37. 83.81 x 6 = _____

38. 22.79 x 3 = _____

39. 11.11 x 7 = _____

40. 55.69 x 2 = _____

33. MULTIPLY A DECIMAL NUMBER BY A DECIMAL NUMBER

Multiply the following numbers:

1. 57.91 x 25.26 = _____

2. 14.23 x 11.12 = _____

3. 26.71 x 15.16 = _____

4. 101.59 x 39.4 = _____

5. 117.19 x 44.45 = _____

6. 114.07 x 43.44 = _____

7. 64.15 x 63.64 = _____

8. 79.75 x 32.33 = _____

9. 85.99 x 34.35 = _____

10. 23.59 x 50.51 = _____

11. 20.47 x 13.14 = _____

12. 110.95 x 42.43 = _____

13. 23.59 x 14.15 = _____

14. 70.39 x 29.3 = _____

15. 61.03 x 26.27 = _____

16. 73.51 x 30.31 = _____

17. 29.83 x 16.17 = _____

18. 17.35 x 48.49 = _____

19. 73.51 x 66.67 = _____

20. 89.11 x 35.36 = _____

21. 14.23 x 47.48 = _____   31. 61.03 x 62.63 = _____

22. 51.67 x 23.24 = _____   32. 51.67 x 59.6 = _____

23. 67.27 x 64.65 = _____   33. 42.31 x 20.21 = _____

24. 11.11 x 46.47 = _____   34. 45.43 x 21.22 = _____

25. 20.47 x 49.5 = _____   35. 29.83 x 52.53 = _____

26. 39.19 x 55.56 = _____   36. 54.79 x 60.61 = _____

27. 26.71 x 51.52 = _____   37. 32.95 x 17.18 = _____

28. 70.39 x 65.66 = _____   38. 36.07 x 54.55 = _____

29. 17.35 x 12.13 = _____   39. 95.35 x 37.38 = _____

30. 104.71 x 40.41 = _____   40. 107.83 x 41.42 = _____

34. MULTIPLY DECIMAL NUMBER BY WHOLE NUMBERS (MISSING FACTOR)

Type the missing factor in the following multiplication equations:

1. _____ x 7 = 302.89

2. _____ x 4 = 103.48

3. _____ x 11 = 151.47

4. _____ x 10 = 441.7

5. _____ x 6 = 179.22

6. _____ x 7 = 321.65

7. _____ x 6 = 163.14

8. _____ x 7 = 331.03

9. _____ x 12 = 324.96

10. _____ x 11 = 164.78

11. _____ x 11 = 138.16

12. _____ x 10 = 417.3

13. _____ x 6 = 171.18

14. _____ x 9 = 243.81

15. _____ x 11 = 124.85

16. _____ x 7 = 312.27

17. _____ x 7 = 340.41

18. _____ x 4 = 113.16

19. _____ x 12 = 339.48

20. _____ x 9 = 254.79

21. _____ x 5 = 214.05

22. _____ x 6 = 187.26

23. _____ x 3 = 34.05

24. _____ x 5 = 201.95

25. _____ x 11 = 178.09

26. _____ x 8 = 89.84

27. _____ x 8 = 119.12

28. _____ x 2 = 83.46

29. _____ x 10 = 453.9

30. _____ x 10 = 429.5

31. _____ x 8 = 109.36

32. _____ x 4 = 122.84

33. _____ x 5 = 226.15

34. _____ x 3 = 37.68

35. _____ x 3 = 41.31

36. _____ x 5 = 208

37. _____ x 2 = 85.9

38. _____ x 2 = 88.34

39. _____ x 4 = 118

40. _____ x 5 = 220.1

35. DECIMAL NUMBERS MULTIPLICATION (WORD PROBLEMS)

1.   Rick's car costs $30,000 and John's car costs $10,000. If they have to buy the car together how much money they need?

2.   John's car gives 30 miles per gallon on the highway. If his car's fuel tank can hold approximate 12 gallons, then how far can he travel on one full tank of gas?

3.   A store owner has 0.92 lbs. of candies in a jar. If she has 10 jars, how much candies do she has in total?

4.   Pavi will pay for his new car in 48 monthly payments. If his car loan is for $21,061, then how much will he pay each month? Round your answer to nearest cent.

5.   Alexandra earns $11.25 per hour for gardening. If she worked 2 hours this week, then how much did she earn?

6.   Akshat ran for a total of 190.6 miles to practice for marathon over 41.5 days. How many miles did he practice on an average per day?

7.   Alex is a clerk in a community bank. He earns $11.50 per hour at the bank. If he worked 2 hours this week, then how much did she earn?

8.   Asha's car gives 30 miles per gallon on a highway. If her car's fuel tank can hold 11.5 gallons, then how far can she travel on one full tank of gas?

9.   A store owner has 19.21 lbs. of candies. If she puts the candy into 10 jars, how much candy will each jar contain?

10. A pizza costs $4 per slice. If there are 2 kids and both wants pizza slice, then how much money is needed to buy one pizza slice for each of them?

11. A member of the school track team ran for a total of 189.6 miles during practice session over 51.5 days. How many miles did he run on an average per day?

12. School lunch costs $10.00 per week. How much would it cost over a period of 10 weeks?

13. Joseph earns $11.75 per hour for gardening. If he worked 33.2 hours this month, then how much did he earn?

14. John's car costs $40,000 and Lisa's car costs $20,000. If they have to buy the car together how much money do, they need to but these cars?

15. Lisa works at grocery store and she earns $11.75 per hour. If she worked 22 hours this week, then how much did she earn?

16. A pizza costs $4 per slice. If there are 3 kids and all of them want a pizza slice, then how much will you spend to feed all of them?

17. At my dad's workplace, lunch is available on subsidized rate. If the lunch costs $10.75 per week. How much money does he need to have lunch over a period 10 weeks?

18. Akshat will pay for his new car in 36 monthly payments. If his car loan is for $25,061, then how much will he pay each month?

36. DIVIDEND, DIVISOR, QUOTIENT, AND REMAINDER

1. What is the divisor in the equation: 56 / 7 = 8?
   a) 56
   b) 7
   c) 8

6. Identify dividend, divisor, quotient in the equation: 44 / 11 = 4
   Divisor   44
   Quotient   11
   Dividend   4

2. What is remainder in the equation: 159 / 11 = 14?
   a) 11
   b) 14
   c) 5

7. What is the divisor in the equation: 110 / 11 = 10?
   110
   11
   10

3. What is the value of dividend in the equation: 2 / 2 = 1?
   a) 2
   b) 2
   c) 1

8. What is remainder in the equation: 62 / 5 = 12?
   a) 5
   b) 12
   c) 2

4. Identify dividend, divisor, quotient in the equation: 32 / 4 = 8
   Divisor   32
   Quotient   4
   Dividend   8

9. What is remainder in the equation: 114 / 12 = 9?

10. What is remainder in the equation: 92 / 8 = 11?

5. What is quotient in the equation: 22 / 2 = 11?
   a) 22
   b) 2
   c) 11

11. What is the value of dividend in the equation: 24 / 8 = 3?
   a) 24
   b) 8
   c) 3

12. What is remainder in the equation: 93 / 11 = 8?

13. What is quotient in the equation: 104 / 8 = 13?
   a) 104
   b) 8
   c) 13

14. What is the value of dividend in the equation: 10 / 5 = 2?
   a) 10
   b) 5
   c) 2

15. What is remainder in the equation: 124 / 8 = 15?
   a) 8
   b) 15
   c) 4

16. What is remainder in the equation: 87 / 7 = 12?

17. Identify dividend, divisor, quotient in the equation: 30 / 5 = 6
   Divisor   30
   Quotient   5
   Dividend   6

18. What is the value of dividend in the equation: 70 / 14 = 5?
   a) 70
   b) 14
   c) 5

19. What is quotient in the equation: 210 / 14 = 15?
   a) 210
   b) 14
   c) 15

20. What is the divisor in the equation: 18 / 3 = 6?
   a) 18
   b) 3
   c) 6

21. What is quotient in the equation: 60 / 5 = 12?
   a) 60
   b) 5
   c) 12

22. What is remainder in the equation: 108 / 8 = 13?
   a) 8
   b) 13
   c) 4

23. Identify dividend, divisor, quotient in the equation: 72 / 9 = 8

      Divisor   72

      Quotient   9

      Dividend   8

24. What is quotient in the equation: 154 / 11 = 14?

a) 154

b) 11

c) 14

25. Identify dividend, divisor, quotient in the equation: 24 / 6 = 4

      Divisor   24

      Quotient   6

      Dividend   4

26. Identify dividend, divisor, quotient in the equation: 84 / 7 = 12

      Divisor   84

      Quotient   7

      Dividend   12

27. What is the divisor in the equation: 81 / 9 = 9?

a) 81

b) 9

c) 9

28. What is remainder in the equation: 94 / 9 = 10?

29. Identify dividend, divisor and quotient in the equation: 24 / 2 = 12

      Divisor   24

      Quotient   2

      Dividend   12

30. What is the value of dividend in the equation: 44 / 11 = 4?

a) 44

b) 11

c) 4

31. Identify dividend, divisor, quotient in the equation: 60 / 10 = 6

      Divisor   60

      Quotient   10

      Dividend   6

32. What is remainder in the equation: 23 / 2 = 11?

a) 2

b) 11

c) 1

33. Identify dividend, divisor, quotient in the equation: 30 / 3 = 10

      Divisor   30

      Quotient   3

      Dividend   10

34. Identify dividend, divisor, quotient in the equation: 80 / 8 = 10

      Divisor   80

      Quotient   8

      Dividend   10

35. What is the divisor in the equation: 35 / 5 = 7?

37.   DIVIDE WHOLE NUMBERS BY 1 DIGIT NUMBERS

Divide the following numbers:

1. 90 / 6 = _____

2. 46 / 2 = _____

3. 90 / 5 = _____

4. 57 / 3 = _____

5. 68 / 4 = _____

6. 138 / 6 = _____

7. 96 / 6 = _____

8. 42 / 3 = _____

9. 84 / 4 = _____

10. 96 / 4 = _____

11. 108 / 6 = _____

12. 50 / 2 = _____

13. 105 / 5 = _____

14. 22 / 2 = _____

15. 72 / 6 = _____

16. 66 / 3 = _____

17. 75 / 5 = _____

18. 100 / 4 = _____

19. 72 / 4 = _____

20. 60 / 5 = _____

21. 42 / 2 = _____   31. 54 / 3 = _____

22. 63 / 3 = _____   32. 110 / 5 = _____

23. 65 / 5 = _____   33. 92 / 4 = _____

24. 114 / 6 = _____   34. 115 / 5 = _____

25. 40 / 2 = _____   35. 78 / 6 = _____

26. 32 / 2 = _____   36. 80 / 4 = _____

27. 120 / 5 = _____   37. 70 / 5 = _____

28. 80 / 5 = _____   38. 48 / 2 = _____

29. 60 / 4 = _____   39. 56 / 4 = _____

30. 34 / 2 = _____   40. 85 / 5 = _____

38. DIVIDE WHOLE NUMBERS BY 2 DIGIT NUMBERS

Divide the following numbers:

1. 240 / 15 = _____

2. 323 / 17 = _____

3. 306 / 17 = _____

4. 182 / 13 = _____

5. 180 / 10 = _____

6. 169 / 13 = _____

7. 224 / 16 = _____

8. 180 / 12 = _____

9. 168 / 14 = _____

10. 208 / 13 = _____

11. 132 / 12 = _____

12. 176 / 11 = _____

13. 156 / 12 = _____

14. 192 / 12 = _____

15. 285 / 15 = _____

16. 204 / 17 = _____

17. 168 / 12 = _____

18. 209 / 11 = _____

19. 225 / 15 = _____

20. 270 / 15 = _____

21. 195 / 13 = _____

22. 165 / 15 = _____

23. 143 / 11 = _____

24. 187 / 11 = _____

25. 154 / 14 = _____

26. 216 / 12 = _____

27. 204 / 12 = _____

28. 266 / 14 = _____

29. 121 / 11 = _____

30. 198 / 11 = _____

31. 208 / 16 = _____

32. 190 / 10 = _____

33. 132 / 11 = _____

34. 240 / 16 = _____

35. 255 / 15 = _____

36. 272 / 16 = _____

37. 130 / 10 = _____

38. 154 / 11 = _____

39. 252 / 14 = _____

40. 110 / 10 = _____

39.   DIVIDE WHOLE NUMBERS BY 10, 100, 1000

1. What is the remainder in the equation: 87 / 10 = 8?

2. What is the quotient in the equation: 1126 / 100 = _____

3. What is the remainder in the equation: 928 / 100 = 9?

4. What is the quotient in the equation: 928 / 100 = _____

5. What is the quotient in the equation: 87 / 10 = _____

6. What is the quotient in the equation: 117 / 10 = _____

7. What is the remainder in the equation: 1027 / 100 = 10?

8. What is the remainder in the equation: 1126 / 100 = 11?

9. What is the quotient in the equation: 126 / 10 = _____

10.   What is the remainder in the equation: 12253 / 1000 = 12?

11.   What is the quotient in the equation: 11251 / 1000 = _____

12.   What is the remainder in the equation: 10252 / 1000 = 10?

13.   What is the remainder in the equation: 9253 / 1000 = 9?

14. What is the quotient in the equation: 1228 / 100 = _____

15. What is the quotient in the equation: 826 / 100 = _____

16. What is the remainder in the equation: 117 / 10 = 11?

17. What is the remainder in the equation: 8251 / 1000 = 8?

18. What is the remainder in the equation: 126 / 10 = 12?

19. What is the quotient in the equation: 96 / 10 = _____

20. What is the quotient in the equation: 108 / 10 = _____

21. What is the quotient in the equation: 9253 / 1000 = _____

22. What is the remainder in the equation: 8500 / 1000 = 8?

23. What is the quotient in the equation: 8251 / 1000 = _____

24. What is the quotient in the equation: 12253 / 1000 = _____

25. What is the remainder in the equation: 1228 / 100 = 12?

26. What is the quotient in the equation: 8500 / 1000 = _____

27. What is the quotient in the equation: 10252 / 1000 = _____

28. What is the remainder in the equation: 108 / 10 = 10?

29. What is the remainder in the equation: 11251 / 1000 = 11?

30. What is the remainder in the equation: 826 / 100 = 8?

31. What is the remainder in the equation: 96 / 10 = 9?

32. What is the quotient in the equation: 1027 / 100 = _____

40. DIVIDE WHOLE NUMBERS ENDING WITH ZERO BY 10, 100, 1000

Divide the following numbers using mental calculation:

1. 12000 / 10 = _____

2. 10000 / 1000 = _____

3. 90 / 10 = _____

4. 80 / 10 = _____

5. 110 / 10 = _____

6. 120 / 10 = _____

7. 23000 / 100 = _____

8. 8500 / 10 = _____

9. 48000 / 1000 = _____

10. 26000 / 100 = _____

11. 29000 / 1000 = _____

12. 13000 / 100 = _____

13. 17000 / 10 = _____

14. 39000 / 100 = _____

15. 12000 / 1000 = _____

16. 1400 / 10 = _____

17. 8000 / 1000 = _____

18. 13000 / 10 = _____

19. 7600 / 10 = _____

20. 2300 / 100 = _____

21. 29000 / 10 = _____

22. 32000 / 100 = _____

23. 3600 / 100 = _____

24. 1500 / 10 = _____

25. 1100 / 100 = _____

26. 4700 / 100 = _____

27. 58000 / 1000 = _____

28. 100 / 10 = _____

29. 5800 / 100 = _____

30. 1300 / 10 = _____

31. 11000 / 1000 = _____

32. 11000 / 10 = _____

41.   DIVISION BY 10S, 100S, 1000S

Divide the following numbers using mental calculation:

1. 40000 / 4000 = _____

2. 450 / 50 = _____

3. 232000 / 80 = _____

4. 23500 / 500 = _____

5. 34000 / 40 = _____

6. 6900 / 300 = _____

7. 104000 / 400 = _____

8. 24000 / 2000 = _____

9. 480 / 60 = _____

10. 288000 / 6000 = _____

11. 104000 / 800 = _____

12. 33000 / 3000 = _____

13. 406000 / 7000 = _____

14. 330 / 30 = _____

15. 145000 / 5000 = _____

16. 2200 / 200 = _____

17. 24000 / 20 = _____

18. 117000 / 300 = _____

19. 38000 / 50 = _____

20. 240 / 20 = _____

21. 1300 / 10 = _____

22. 34800 / 600 = _____

23. 14400 / 400 = _____

24. 64000 / 200 = _____

25. 2800 / 20 = _____

26. 161000 / 700 = _____

27. 8000 / 1000 = _____

28. 65000 / 50 = _____

29. 4500 / 30 = _____

30. 400 / 40 = _____

31. 119000 / 70 = _____

32. 33000 / 30 = _____

42.   SIMPLE DIVISION (WORD PROBLEMS)

1.   Usha takes 10 minutes to read 100 cards. How long will she take to read 1000 cards?

2.   How many days' will 30 pounds of meat last if a fox in a zoo eats 3 pounds of meat per day?

3.   Usha collected 100 different kind of flowers during spring. If she made a bouquet with 20 flowers, how many bouquets she can make?

4.   Akshat has to do 100 math problems. If he can do 10 problems per minute, then how much time will he take to complete all of them?

5.   A tiger eats 15 pounds of meat daily. How long will 225 pounds of meat last?

6.   A school took kids on a field trip. Each teacher was responsible to manage and look after 20 kids. How many teachers will be required to manage 160 kids?

7.   A kid takes 1 minute to solve 10 problems in his class. How long will he take to solve 100 problems?

8.   A tray can hold 121 eggs. If there are 11 rows in a tray, then how many columns are there?

9.   A tiger eats 1 pound of meat in 1 minute. How long will he take to eat 10 pounds?

10.   A chef cooks 25 pounds of food every day in a restaurant. Over how many days' he will cook 1250 pounds of food?

11. A person eats .3 Kg of vegetables every day. How many days' will 3 kg of vegetables last?

12. Usha takes 10 minutes to sort 100 cards. How long will she take to sort 1000 cards?

13. If you buy about 12 pounds of fruits on weekly basis. Over how many weeks' you will buy 240 pounds of fruits?

43.   DIVIDE WHOLE NUMBER BY 1 DIGIT NUMBER HAVING DECIMAL QUOTIENTS

Divide the following numbers and show the result to 2 decimal places:

1. 135 / 6 = _____

2. 41 / 2 = _____

3. 98 / 6 = _____

4. 49 / 4 = _____

5. 82 / 5 = _____

6. 73 / 6 = _____

7. 171 / 7 = _____

8. 35 / 2 = _____

9. 66 / 5 = _____

10. 104 / 6 = _____

11. 57 / 4 = _____

12. 66 / 4 = _____

13. 78 / 7 = _____

14. 65 / 3 = _____

15. 118 / 5 = _____

16. 118 / 9 = _____

17. 62 / 3 = _____

18. 71 / 5 = _____

19. 91 / 6 = _____

20. 85 / 6 = _____

21. 99 / 7 = _____

22. 142 / 7 = _____

23. 25 / 2 = _____

24. 78 / 4 = _____

25. 100 / 9 = _____

26. 99 / 4 = _____

27. 92 / 7 = _____

28. 74 / 3 = _____

29. 74 / 4 = _____

30. 37 / 3 = _____

31. 203 / 8 = _____

32. 47 / 2 = _____

33. 106 / 7 = _____

34. 155 / 9 = _____

35. 71 / 3 = _____

36. 76 / 5 = _____

37. 29 / 2 = _____

38. 45 / 2 = _____

39. 50 / 3 = _____

40. 219 / 9 = _____

44. DIVIDE WHOLE NUMBER BY 2 DIGIT NUMBER HAVING DECIMAL QUOTIENTS

Divide the following numbers and show the result to 2 decimal places:

1. 144 / 10 = _____

2. 200 / 13 = _____

3. 198 / 12 = _____

4. 144 / 13 = _____

5. 159 / 12 = _____

6. 199 / 10 = _____

7. 211 / 12 = _____

8. 159 / 13 = _____

9. 211 / 16 = _____

10. 170 / 11 = _____

11. 332 / 17 = _____

12. 123 / 10 = _____

13. 182 / 11 = _____

14. 262 / 16 = _____

15. 188 / 17 = _____

16. 185 / 14 = _____

17. 185 / 12 = _____

18. 246 / 15 = _____

19. 122 / 11 = _____

20. 206 / 11 = _____

21. 147 / 12 = _____

22. 158 / 11 = _____

23. 214 / 13 = _____

24. 172 / 12 = _____

25. 256 / 13 = _____

26. 146 / 11 = _____

27. 260 / 14 = _____

28. 228 / 16 = _____

29. 262 / 15 = _____

30. 111 / 10 = _____

31. 171 / 14 = _____

32. 207 / 17 = _____

33. 166 / 15 = _____

34. 195 / 16 = _____

35. 133 / 10 = _____

36. 194 / 11 = _____

37. 278 / 15 = _____

38. 245 / 14 = _____

39. 133 / 12 = _____

40. 224 / 12 = _____

45. DIVIDE WHOLE NUMBER BY WHOLE NUMBER HAVING REMAINDER

1. What is the quotient and remainder in 23 / 7
   a) 3
   b) 2
   c) 4
   d) 6

2. What is the quotient and remainder in 18 / 4
   a) 4
   b) 2
   c) 5
   d) 6

3. What is the quotient and remainder in 49 / 9
   a) 5
   b) 4
   c) 6
   d) 8

4. What is the quotient and remainder in 20 / 8
   a) 2
   b) 4
   c) 3
   d) 7

5. What is the quotient and remainder in 49 / 11
   a) 4
   b) 5
   c) 6
   d) 9

6. What is the quotient and remainder in 38 / 11
   a) 3
   b) 5
   c) 4
   d) 9

7. What is the quotient and remainder in 18 / 7
   a) 2
   b) 4
   c) 3
   d) 7

8. What is the quotient and remainder in 28 / 8
   a) 3
   b) 4
   c) 5
   d) 8

9. What is the quotient and remainder in 54 / 12
   a) 4
   b) 6
   c) 5
   d) 10

10. What is the quotient and remainder in 45 / 13
   a) 3
   b) 6
   c) 4
   d) 10

11. What is the quotient and remainder in 58 / 13
   a) 4
   b) 6
   c) 5
   d) 10

12. What is the quotient and remainder in 66 / 12
   a) 5
   b) 6
   c) 7
   d) 10

13. What is the quotient and remainder in 5 / 2
   a) 2
   b) 1
   c) 4
   d) 5

14. What is the quotient and remainder in 10 / 3
   a) 3
   b) 1
   c) 4
   d) 5

15. What is the quotient and remainder in 27 / 11
   a) 2
   b) 5
   c) 3
   d) 8

16. What is the quotient and remainder in 25 / 10
   a) 2
   b) 5
   c) 3
   d) 8

17. What is the quotient and remainder in 27 / 5
   a) 5
   b) 2
   c) 6
   d) 7

18. What is the quotient and remainder in 31 / 9
   a) 3
   b) 4
   c) 5
   d) 8

19. What is the quotient and remainder in 9 / 4
   a) 2
   b) 1
   c) 3
   d) 4

20. What is the quotient and remainder in 32 / 13
   a) 2
   b) 6
   c) 3
   d) 9

21. What is the quotient and remainder in 17 / 5
a) 3
b) 2
c) 4
d) 6

22. What is the quotient and remainder in 45 / 10
a) 4
b) 5
c) 6
d) 9

23. What is the quotient and remainder in 31 / 7
a) 4
b) 3
c) 5
d) 7

24. What is the quotient and remainder in 33 / 6
a) 5
b) 3
c) 6
d) 7

25. What is the quotient and remainder in 42 / 12
a) 3
b) 6
c) 4
d) 10

26. What is the quotient and remainder in 7 / 2
a) 3
b) 1
c) 4
d) 5

27. What is the quotient and remainder in 38 / 7
a) 5
b) 3
c) 6
d) 7

28. What is the quotient and remainder in 14 / 4
a) 3
b) 2
c) 4
d) 6

29. What is the quotient and remainder in 59 / 11
a) 5
b) 4
c) 6
d) 8

30. What is the quotient and remainder in 16 / 6
a) 2
b) 4
c) 3
d) 7

31. What is the quotient and remainder in 71 / 13
   a) 5
   b) 6
   c) 7
   d) 10

32. What is the quotient and remainder in 35 / 8
   a) 4
   b) 3
   c) 5
   d) 7

33. What is the quotient and remainder in 27 / 6
   a) 4
   b) 3
   c) 5
   d) 7

34. What is the quotient and remainder in 16 / 3
   a) 5
   b) 1
   c) 6
   d) 7

35. What is the quotient and remainder in 13 / 3
   a) 4
   b) 1
   c) 6
   d) 5

36. What is the quotient and remainder in 39 / 9
   a) 4
   b) 3
   c) 5
   d) 7

37. What is the quotient and remainder in 22 / 9
   a) 2
   b) 4
   c) 3
   d) 7

38. What is the quotient and remainder in 44 / 8
   a) 5
   b) 4
   c) 6
   d) 8

39. What is the quotient and remainder in 22 / 5
   a) 4
   b) 2
   c) 5
   d) 6

40. What is the quotient and remainder in 9 / 2
   a) 4
   b) 1
   c) 6
   d) 5

46.   DIVIDE DECIMAL NUMBERS BY WHOLE NUMBER HAVING DECIMAL QUOTIENTS

Divide the following numbers and show the result to 2 decimal places:

1.   152.88 / 8 = _____

2.   240.44 / 11 = _____

3.   47.77 / 3 = _____

4.   32.18 / 2 = _____

5.   73.08 / 4 = _____

6.   68.05 / 5 = _____

7.   78.2 / 3 = _____

8.   203.67 / 13 = _____

9.   73.5 / 5 = _____

10.   53.98 / 2 = _____

11.   261 / 10 = _____

12.   237.2 / 10 = _____

13.   34.36 / 2 = _____

14.   65.12 / 3 = _____

15.   121.7 / 6 = _____

16.   81.8 / 4 = _____

17.   125.72 / 8 = _____

18.   213.4 / 10 = _____

19.   107.2 / 5 = _____

20.   188.48 / 11 = _____

21.   94.54 / 6 = _____   31.   110.13 / 7 = _____

22.   144.16 / 8 = _____   32.   241.41 / 9 = _____

23.   113.65 / 5 = _____   33.   74.93 / 3 = _____

24.   119.1 / 5 = _____   34.   115.16 / 6 = _____

25.   87.24 / 7 = _____   35.   41.23 / 3 = _____

26.   37.96 / 3 = _____   36.   322.88 / 12 = _____

27.   57.15 / 5 = _____   37.   38.72 / 2 = _____

28.   34.69 / 3 = _____   38.   140.76 / 12 = _____

29.   86.16 / 4 = _____   39.   131.5 / 9 = _____

30.   102.5 / 7 = _____   40.   197.5 / 13 = _____

47.   DIVISION PATTERNS

Complete the following division patterns using given hints:

1. If 45 / 9= 5   Then 4500 / 9 = _____

2. If 42 / 2= 21   Then 4200 / 2 = _____

3. If 216 / 9= 24   Then 216000 / 9 =

_____

4. If 102 / 6= 17   Then 10200 / 6 =

_____

5. If 28 / 7= 4   Then 2800 / 7 = _____

6. If 45 / 9= 5   Then 450 / 9 = _____

7. If 120 / 15= 8   Then 1200 / 15 =

_____

11. If 28 / 7= 4   Then 280 / 7 = _____

12. If 28 / 7= 4   Then 28000 / 7 = _____

13. If 6 / 3= 2   Then 6000 / 3 = _____

14. If 190 / 19= 10   Then 1900 / 19 =

_____

15. If 132 / 11= 12   Then 13200 / 11 =

_____

16. If 90 / 5= 18   Then 9000 / 5 = _____

17. If 116 / 4= 29   Then 116000 / 4 =

_____

8. If 62 / 2= 31   Then 62000 / 2 = _____

18. If 200 / 8= 25   Then 200000 / 8 =

9. If 162 / 6= 27   Then 162000 / 6 =

_____

19. If 66 / 11= 6   Then 66000 / 11 =

10. If 231 / 21= 11   Then 231000 / 21 =   _____

_____

20. If 120 / 8= 15   Then 12000 / 8 =

_____

21. If 15 / 5= 3   Then 150 / 5 = _____

31. If 126 / 9= 14   Then 12600 / 9 =

22. If 153 / 17= 9   Then 1530 / 17 =

_____

32. If 60 / 3= 20   Then 6000 / 3 = _____

_____

23. If 120 / 15= 8   Then 12000 / 15 =

33. If 190 / 19= 10   Then 19000 / 19 =

_____

_____

24. If 231 / 21= 11   Then 23100 / 21 =

_____

25. If 66 / 11= 6   Then 660 / 11 = _____

26. If 190 / 19= 10   Then 190000 / 19 =

_____

27. If 112 / 7= 16   Then 11200 / 7 =

_____

28. If 15 / 5= 3   Then 1500 / 5 = _____

29. If 182 / 7= 26   Then 182000 / 7 =

_____

34. If 6 / 3= 2   Then 60 / 3 = _____

35. If 91 / 13= 7   Then 91000 / 13 =

_____

36. If 242 / 11= 22   Then 242000 / 11 =

_____

37. If 6 / 3= 2   Then 600 / 3 = _____

38. If 153 / 17= 9   Then 15300 / 17 =

_____

39. If 91 / 13= 7   Then 910 / 13 = _____

40. If 66 / 11= 6   Then 6600 / 11 = _____

30. If 90 / 3 = 30   Then 90000 / 3 =

_____

48.   DIVISION PROBLEMS (TRUE OR FALSE)

Verify each of the following statement whether it is correct (true) or not (false):

1. Is 120 / 12 < 10
    a) False
    b) True

2. Is 130 / 13 = 10
    a) True
    b) False

3. Is 30 / 3 > 10
    a) False
    b) True

4. Is 36 / 4 > 9
    a) False
    b) True

5. Is 36 / 4 = 9
    a) True
    b) False

6. Is 108 / 12 = 9
    a) True
    b) False

7. Is 45 / 5 > 9
    a) False
    b) True

8. Is 150 / 15 > 10
    a) False
    b) True

9. Is 60 / 6 = 10
    a) True
    b) False

10. Is 171 / 19 > 9
    a) False
    b) True

11. Is 30 / 3 = 10
    a) True
    b) False

12. Is 18 / 2 = 9
    a) True
    b) False

13. Is 171 / 19 = 9
    a) True
    b) False

14. Is 60 / 6 > 10
    a) False
    b) True

15. Is 81 / 9 = 9
   a) True
   b) False

16. Is 117 / 13 < 9
   a) False
   b) True

17. Is 126 / 14 = 9
   a) True
   b) False

18. Is 190 / 19 > 10
   a) False
   b) True

19. Is 190 / 19 = 10
   a) True
   b) False

20. Is 108 / 12 < 9
   a) False
   b) True

21. Is 130 / 13 < 10
   a) False
   b) True

22. Is 90 / 9 > 10
   a) False
   b) True

23. Is 20 / 2 = 10
   a) True
   b) False

24. Is 130 / 13 > 10
   a) False
   b) True

25. Is 18 / 2 < 9
   a) False
   b) True

26. Is 63 / 7 < 9
   a) False
   b) True

27. Is 45 / 5 = 9
   a) True
   b) False

28. Is 81 / 9 < 9
   a) False
   b) True

29. Is 63 / 7 > 9
   a) False
   b) True

30. Is 160 / 16 = 10
   a) True
   b) False

31. Is 126 / 14 > 9
   a) False
   b) True

32. Is 117 / 13 = 9
   a) True
   b) False

33. Is 90 / 9 < 10
   a) False
   b) True

34. Is 20 / 2 > 10
   a) False
   b) True

35. Is 50 / 5 = 10
   a) True
   b) False

36. Is 63 / 7 = 9
   a) True
   b) False

37. Is 120 / 12 > 10
   a) False
   b) True

38. Is 40 / 4 < 10
   a) False
   b) True

39. Is 27 / 3 = 9
   a) True
   b) False

40. Is 140 / 14 > 10
   a) False
   b) True

49. DIVISION PROBLEMS (MISSING NUMBER)

Type the missing number:

1. 30 / _____ = 6

2. 21 / _____ = 3

3. 4 / _____ = 1

4. 65 / 5 = _____

5. 8 / 8 = _____

6. 77 / 11 = _____

7. 44 / _____ = 11

8. 48 / _____ = 8

9. 60 / 5 = _____

10. 70 / 14 = _____

11. 96 / 12 = _____

12. 54 / _____ = 9

13. 50 / 10 = _____

14. 20 / 2 = _____

15. 96 / _____ = 12

16. 18 / 2 = _____

17. 70 / _____ = 14

18. 32 / 4 = _____

19. 66 / 11 = _____

20. 60 / 10 = _____

21. 39 / _____ = 13

22. 42 / _____ = 6

23. 32 / 16 = _____

24. 42 / 14 = _____

25. 68 / 17 = _____

26. 18 / _____ = 6

27. 22 / _____ = 11

28. 91 / _____ = 13

29. 80 / 10 = _____

30. 36 / _____ = 9

31. 65 / _____ = 13

32. 5 / 5 = _____

33. 84 / 7 = _____

34. 16 / 2 = _____

35. 48 / 6 = _____

36. 21 / 7 = _____

37. 72 / 8 = _____

38. 25 / 5 = _____

39. 26 / 13 = _____

40. 60 / 6 = _____

ANSWERS KEY

1.Mathematical Problems using Even and Odd Numbers	2.Negative and Positive Numbers (Sorting Order)	
1. Odd	1. False	27. -22
2. Even	2. -3 is the middle number	28. False
3. Even	2. -1 is the biggest number	29. True
4. Even	2. -13 is the smallest number	30. False
5. Odd	3. -12 is the middle number	31. -21
6. Even	3. -6 is the biggest number	32. -18 is the middle number
7. Even	3. -15 is the smallest number	32. -15 is the biggest number
8. Even	4. False	32. -19 is the smallest number
9. Even	5. False	33. True
10. Odd	6. True	34. -9 is the middle number
11. Even	7. -15 is the middle number	34. -4 is the biggest number
12. Odd	7. -2 is the biggest number	34. -14 is the smallest number
13. Even	7. -19 is the smallest number	35. False
14. Even	8. False	36. -2
15. Odd	9. -12	37. False
16. Odd	10. False	38. False
17. Even	11. False	39. True
18. Odd	12. True	40. -10
19. Even	13. False	
20. Even	14. -4	
21. Even	15. True	
22. Odd	16. -19	
23. Even	17. True	
24. Even	18. True	
25. Odd	19. False	
26. Even	20. -4 is the middle number	
27. Odd	20. -1 is the biggest number	
28. Even	20. -14 is the smallest number	
29. Odd	21. False	
30. Odd	22. True	
31. Odd	23. -17 is the middle number	
32. Even	23. -15 is the biggest number	
33. Even	23. -19 is the smallest number	
34. Even	24. -14 is the middle number	
35. Even	24. -2 is the biggest number	
36. Even	24. -19 is the smallest number	
37. Even	25. True	
38. Even	26. -8 is the middle number	
39. Even	26. -4 is the biggest number	
40. Even	26. -14 is the smallest number	

3.Numbers Review (True or False)

1. True
2. True
3. True
4. False
5. False
6. True
7. True
9. False
11. True
12. True
13. False
14. False
15. False
16. True
18. False
19. False
20. False
21. False
23. True
24. True
25. True
26. True
27. False
28. False
29. True
30. False
31. True
32. False
33. False
34. True
35. False
36. False
37. False
38. True
39. False
40. True

4.Addition and Subtraction (Missing Numbers)

1. 309555
2. 7971
3. 176617
4. 188920
5. 60388
6. 241370
7. 246615
8. 288575
9. 17087
10. 21645
11. 12529
12. 42156
13. 58109
14. 204655
15. 39877
16. 299065
17. 64946
18. 236125
19. 26203
20. 35319
21. 80899
22. 28482
23. 194165
24. 362005
25. 304310
26. 67225
27. 351515
28. 174338
29. 341025
30. 10250
31. 199410
32. 5692
33. 14808
34. 37598
35. 178896
36. 62667
37. 293820
38. 23924
39. 172059
40. 19366

5.Addition and Subtraction (Word Problems)

1. 12
2. 63
3. 78
4. 8
5. 49
6. 87
7. 22
8. 56
9. 29
10. 7
11. 13
12. 86
13. 45
14. 79
15. 50
16. 45
17. 26
18. 60
19. 44
20. 89
21. 54
22. 53

6.Rounding and Estimate Numbers

1. 180
2. 320
3. 300
4. 430
5. 410
6. 60
7. 380
8. 240
9. 350
10. 450
11. 380
12. 340
13. 90
14. 150
15. 470
16. 300
17. 30
18. 270
19. 120
20. 320
21. 200
22. 360
23. 30

7.Addition and Subtraction Facts using Decimal Numbers	8.Add and Subtract Decimal Numbers (Missing Numbers)	9.Add and Subtract Decimal Numbers (Word Problems)
1. 339815.6	1. 39198.59	1. 1.89
2. 347339.63	2. 60609.86	2. 1.5
3. 415055.9	3. 13029.26	3. 0.86
4. 61426.49	4. 65367.92	4. 1.88
5. 211907.09	5. 17787.32	5. 1.9
6. 144190.82	6. 22545.38	6. 1.81
7. 38854.4	7. 43956.65	7. 1.7
8. 430103.96	8. 62988.89	8. 1.88
9. 204383.06	9. 70125.98	9. 0.85
10. 219431.12	10. 67746.95	10. 1.85
11. 369911.72	11. 15408.29	11. 0.9
12. 196859.03	12. 41577.62	12. 1.83
13. 272099.33	13. 36819.56	13. 1.63
14. 121618.73	14. 20166.35	14. 0.88
15. 46378.43	15. 84400.16	15. 0.89
16. 114094.7	16. 189028.83	
17. 136666.79	17. 46335.68	
18. 264575.3		
19. 354863.66		
20. 422579.93		
21. 287147.39		
22. 53902.46		
23. 68950.52		
24. 189335		
25. 279623.36		
26. 129142.76		
27. 294671.42		
28. 362387.69		

10. Compare and Balance Equations using Decimal Numbers	11. Rounding and Estimate Decimal Numbers	12. Multiply by 1 Digit Numbers
1. <	1. 353	1. 190
2. =	2. 265	2. 192
3. =	3. 89	3. 200
4. >	4. 118	4. 63
5. <	5. 148	5. 290
6. <	6. 405	6. 189
7. =	7. 31	7. 56
8. =	8. 324	8. 340
9. >	9. 469	9. 315
10. <	10. 1	10. 156
11. =	11. 320	11. 204
12. =	12. 206	12. 150
13. =	13. 447	13. 108
14. <	14. 341	14. 203
15. =	15. 362	15. 234
16. =	16. 382	16. 119
17. >	17. 236	17. 224
18. =	18. 177	18. 192
19. =	19. 294	19. 175
20. <	20. 383	20. 165
21. =	21. 298	21. 144
22. <	22. 426	22. 265
23. =	23. 60	23. 365
24. >		24. 96
25. =		25. 318
26. >		26. 136
27. =		27. 168
28. >		28. 217
29. <		29. 402
30. <		30. 81
31. >		31. 135
32. =		32. 72
33. >		33. 215
34. =		34. 133
35. <		35. 272
36. <		36. 152
37. =		37. 296
38. <		38. 105
39. >		39. 528
40. =		40. 248

13.Multiply by 2 Digit Numbers	14.Multipley 10s, 100s and 1000s by 1 Digit Numbers	15.Multipley 10s, 100s and 1000s by 2 Digit Numbers
1. 2336	1. 240	1. 9900
2. 3770	2. 30	2. 990
3. 966	3. 60	3. 132000
4. 260	4. 5600	4. 480
5. 1590	5. 200	5. 110
6. 2318	6. 6400	6. 11000
7. 777	7. 96000	7. 495000
8. 4158	8. 140	8. 7700
9. 544	9. 240	9. 770
10. 552	10. 100	10. 5500
11. 1836	11. 350	11. 330
12. 3078	12. 144000	12. 550
13. 286	13. 3000	13. 240
14. 2028	14. 420	14. 253000
15. 648	15. 250	
16. 1470	16. 280	
17. 924	17. 1200	
18. 1353	18. 32000	
19. 1800	19. 45000	
20. 1798	20. 84000	
21. 2244	21. 60000	
22. 1200	22. 28000	
23. 1128	23. 120	
24. 2640	24. 1400	
25. 1278	25. 1000	
26. 1334	26. 2400	
27. 390	27. 39000	
28. 820	28. 65000	
29. 154	29. 8400	
30. 408	30. 56000	
31. 2025	31. 91000	
32. 5382	32. 140	
33. 110	33. 50	
34. 1512	34. 480	
35. 2430	35. 210	
36. 1980	36. 3000	
37. 322	37. 120	
38. 630	38. 440	
39. 2666	39. 6000	
40. 204	40. 9600	

16.Properties of Multiplication	15. Identity Property 2 x 1 = 2	17.Multiplication and Distributive Properties
1. Identity Property 7 x 1 = 7	15. Associative Property 2 x (6 x 10) = (2 x 6) x 10	1. 14
1. Associative Property 7 x (10 x 16) = (7 x 10) x 16	15. Commutative Property 2 x (6 x 10) = (6 x 10) x 2	2. 18
1. Commutative Property 7 x (10 x 16) = (10 x 16) x 7	16. Identity Property 6 x 1 = 6	3. 6
2. 8 x 1 = 8	16. Associative Property 6 x (9 x 14) = (6 x 9) x 14	4. 2
3. 12 x 1 = 12	16. Commutative Property 6 x (9 x 14) = (9 x 14) x 6	5. 9
4. Identity Property 11 x 1 = 11	17. 11 x 1 = 11	6. 2
4. Associative Property 11 x (9 x 13) = (11 x 9) x 13	18. Identity Property 4 x 1 = 4	7. 20
4. Commutative Property 11 x (9 x 13) = (9 x 13) x 11	18. Associative Property 4 x (7 x 10) = (4 x 7) x 10	8. 10
5. 9 x 1 = 9	18. Commutative Property 4 x (7 x 10) = (7 x 10) x 4	9. 2
6. 9 x (12 x 13) = (9 x 12) x 13	20. 13 x (18 x 23) = (13 x 18) x 23	10. 6
7. 9 x (12 x 13) = (12 x 13) x 9	21. Identity Property 3 x 1 = 3	11. 10
8. 11 x (14 x 24) = (14 x 24) x 11	21. Associative Property 3 x (6 x 8) = (3 x 6) x 8	12. 8
9. 12 x (15 x 26) = (15 x 26) x 12	21. Commutative Property 3 x (6 x 8) = (6 x 8) x 3	13. 3
10. Identity Property 5 x 1 = 5	22. 11 x (15 x 18) = (11 x 15) x 18	14. 21
10. Associative Property 5 x (7 x 11) = (5 x 7) x 11	23. 15 x (21 x 28) = (15 x 21) x 28	15. 4
10. Commutative Property 5 x (7 x 11) = (7 x 11) x 5	24. 13 x (18 x 23) = (18 x 23) x 13	16. 13
11. Identity Property 14 x 1 = 14	25. 17 x (24 x 33) = (17 x 24) x 33	17. 11
11. Associative Property 14 x (10 x 14) = (14 x 10) x 14		18. 7
11. Commutative Property 14 x (10 x 14) = (10 x 14) x 14		19. 11
12. Identity Property 5 x 1 = 5		20. 9
12. Associative Property 5 x (8 x 12) = (5 x 8) x 12		21. 3
12. Commutative Property 5 x (8 x 12) = (8 x 12) x 5		22. 4
13. Identity Property 8 x 1 = 8		23. 4
13. Associative Property 8 x (8 x 12) = (8 x 8) x 12		24. 12
13. Commutative Property 8 x (8 x 12) = (8 x 12) x 8		25. 1
14. 10 x (13 x 22) = (10 x 13) x 22		26. 27
		27. 7
		28. 24
		29. 1
		30. 18
		31. 4
		32. 13
		33. 8
		34. 5
		35. 7
		36. 5
		37. 12
		38. 8
		39. 12
		40. 5

18.Rounding and Multiplication	19.Multiply by 1 and 2 Digit Numbers (Missing Factor)	20.Multiply by 1 and 2 Digit Numbers (True or False)
1. 5400	1. 15	1. True
2. 2400	2. 16	2. True
3. 1000	3. 16	3. True
4. 1400	4. 11	4. True
5. 3600	5. 15	5. True
6. 1000	6. 3	6. True
7. 2700	7. 14	7. True
8. 5400	8. 5	8. True
9. 500	9. 2	9. True
10. 1600	10. 4	10. True
11. 2400	11. 12	11. True
12. 1800	12. 13	12. True
13. 2800	13. 12	13. True
14. 2700	14. 11	14. False
15. 400	15. 6	15. True
16. 400	16. 12	16. True
17. 2700	17. 17	17. True
18. 5400	18. 11	18. True
19. 700	19. 3	19. True
20. 1800	20. 2	20. True
21. 1400	21. 5	21. True
22. 2800	22. 10	22. True
23. 600	23. 10	23. True
24. 1600	24. 2	24. True
25. 2100	25. 12	25. True
26. 700	26. 6	26. True
27. 4000	27. 16	27. True
28. 2400	28. 8	28. True
29. 1200	29. 7	29. True
30. 3600	30. 16	30. True
31. 4500	31. 17	31. True
32. 700	32. 8	32. True
33. 4000	33. 9	33. True
34. 1600	34. 13	34. True
35. 1400	35. 8	35. True
36. 1600	36. 13	36. True
37. 3200	37. 14	37. True
38. 3600	38. 18	38. True
39. 1800	39. 17	39. True
40. 2700	40. 3	40. True

21.Multiply by 1 and 2 Digit Numbers (Word Problems)	22.Identify Multiplicand, Multiplier and Products	23.Multiply 3 Digit Number by 1 Digit Number
1. 784	1. 21	1. 1419
2. 880 miles	2. 108	2. 2420
3. 700	3. Multiplicand 6	3. 3592
4. 140	3. Multiplier 9	4. 1455
5. $360 worth of meat	3. Product 54	5. 1563
6. 700	4. 24	6. 4072
7. $360 worth of meat	5. 11	7. 822
8. 130	6. 12	8. 3745
9. 741	7. Multiplicand 2	9. 5985
10. 5980	7. Multiplier 6	10. 113
	7. Product 12	11. 1167
	8. Multiplicand 8	12. 3784
	8. Multiplier 8	13. 1967
	8. Product 64	14. 1203
	9. 12	15. 2372
	10. Multiplicand 4	16. 3385
	10. Multiplier 7	17. 658
	10. Product 28	18. 606
	11. 18	19. 2303
	13. 15	20. 5229
	14. 9	21. 221
	15. Multiplicand 5	22. 125
	15. Multiplier 8	23. 3985
	15. Product 40	24. 4168
	16. 8	25. 209
	17. Multiplicand 5	26. 514
	17. Multiplier 7	27. 1110
	17. Product 35	28. 2132
	18. Multiplicand 14	29. 2660
	18. Multiplier 10	30. 1326
	18. Product 140	31. 3304
	19. Multiplicand 3	32. 185
	19. Multiplier 6	33. 562
	19. Product 18	34. 586
	20. 234	35. 1883
	21. Multiplicand 11	36. 750
	21. Multiplier 9	37. 1715
	21. Product 99	38. 5769
	22. Multiplicand 7	39. 3805
	22. Multiplier 10	40. 149
	22. Product 70	
	23. 13	
	24. 154	
	25. 180	

24.Multiply 3 Digit Number by 2 Digit Number	25.Multiply 3 Digit Number by 3 Digit Number	26.Multiply 3 Whole Numbers
1. 18642	1. 57720	1. 1071
2. 6860	2. 60138	2. 54
3. 11070	3. 25506	3. 690
4. 14910	4. 56238	4. 480
5. 8466	5. 54418	5. 336
6. 20664	6. 26650	6. 225
7. 21714	7. 94572	7. 1152
8. 23892	8. 40248	8. 1200
9. 11990	9. 27924	9. 360
10. 1820	10. 25194	10. 1365
11. 10092	11. 24024	11. 1176
12. 5124	12. 26650	12. 138
13. 10830	13. 49764	13. 1710
14. 18056	14. 81260	14. 507
15. 6210	15. 56238	15. 1683
16. 22790	16. 57015	16. 600
17. 25058	17. 59670	17. 600
18. 21440	18. 88592	18. 1440
19. 2142	19. 40400	19. 264
20. 16724	20. 28054	20. 342
21. 2490	21. 49764	21. 156
22. 19640	22. 43758	22. 924
23. 3264	23. 40248	23. 480
24. 27600	24. 72576	24. 1650
25. 6792	25. 59670	25. 1536
26. 4142	26. 25194	26. 1440
27. 28910	27. 58864	27. 672
28. 7400	28. 23634	28. 210
29. 14906	29. 57720	29. 768
30. 13908	30. 26416	30. 1176
31. 15930	31. 27846	31. 1008
32. 9380	32. 27300	32. 1197
33. 13200	33. 27300	33. 672
34. 25020	34. 24024	34. 150
35. 11594	35. 25506	35. 480
36. 6096	36. 77087	36. 798
37. 26316	37. 28054	37. 276
38. 1010	38. 52260	38. 240
39. 20286	39. 54418	39. 561
40. 17670	40. 27456	40. 975

27.Multiply 3 Whole Numbers (Missing Numbers)	28.Multiply 4 Digit Number by 3 Digit Number	29. Multiplication Patterns
1. 10	1. 266344	1. 45000
2. 4	2. 565928	2. 600
3. 10	3. 1161576	3. 4500
4. 2	4. 512652	4. 19000
5. 9	5. 246636	5. 2310
6. 6	6. 258258	6. 200000
7. 1	7. 698807	7. 11200
8. 5	8. 234234	8. 230000
9. 5	9. 399672	9. 162000
10. 7	10. 657504	10. 231000
11. 6	11. 1404208	11. 1200
12. 2	12. 531570	12. 182000
13. 4	13. 551616	13. 150
14. 7	14. 238212	14. 1500
15. 7	15. 515655	15. 190000
16. 7	16. 1338870	16. 6600
17. 1	17. 256048	17. 9100
18. 8	18. 263796	18. 10200
19. 3	19. 613211	19. 28000
20. 2	20. 850278	20. 66000
21. 8	21. 479076	21. 660
22. 2	22. 1466556	22. 120000
23. 10	23. 367224	23. 910
24. 3	24. 1124916	24. 216000
25. 6	25. 223704	25. 7600
26. 9	26. 499564	26. 4200
27. 6	27. 557154	27. 13200
28. 4	28. 737120	28. 1900
29. 3	29. 966004	29. 450
30. 5	30. 517062	30. 12600
31. 9	31. 1199224	31. 242000
32. 3	32. 772443	32. 60
33. 8	33. 804776	33. 23100
34. 4	34. 262470	34. 12000
35. 4	35. 1069770	35. 15000
36. 10	36. 654264	36. 12000
37. 1	37. 429130	37. 1530
38. 5	38. 834119	38. 6000
39. 4	39. 647006	39. 153000
40. 8	40. 455598	40. 9000

30.Multiply 10s, 100s, 1000s by Decimal Numbers	31.Decimal Numbers Multiplication (True or False)	32.Multiply a Decimal Number by 1 Digit Whole Number
1. 108000	1. False	1. 190.41
2. 2268	2. True	2. 75.72
3. 25	3. True	3. 311.85
4. 818.4	4. False	4. 22.5
5. 72	5. True	5. 197.65
6. 4670	6. False	6. 136.74
7. 27690	7. True	7. 166.04
8. 637.7	8. False	8. 103.3
9. 276240	9. False	9. 278.45
10. 62720	10. False	10. 95.22
11. 499.2	11. True	11. 129.56
12. 105090	12. False	12. 68.76
13. 86800	13. False	13. 197.76
14. 7806	14. False	14. 30.58
15. 131400	15. True	15. 37.86
16. 232	16. True	16. 563.88
17. 56700	17. True	17. 380.82
18. 345	18. False	18. 162.89
19. 1240	19. False	19. 220.92
20. 11676	20. True	20. 56.6
21. 211850	21. True	21. 93.08
22. 2700	22. False	22. 157.25
23. 21618	23. False	23. 205.45
24. 16280	24. False	24. 159.9
25. 141	25. True	25. 258.78
26. 1021.5	26. True	26. 319.8
27. 154880	27. True	27. 79.06
28. 4380	28. False	28. 44.44
	29. False	29. 226.73
	30. True	30. 62.9
	31. True	31. 76.45
	32. True	32. 220.92
	33. True	33. 105.24
	34. True	34. 269.29
	35. True	35. 281.94
	36. True	36. 141.72
	37. False	37. 502.86
	38. True	38. 68.37
	39. True	39. 77.77
	40. True	40. 111.38

33.Multiply a Decimal Number by a Decimal Number	34.Multiply Decimal Number by Whole Numbers (Missing Factor)	35.Decimal Numbers Multiplication (Word Problems)
1. 1462.81	1. 43.27	1. 40000
2. 158.2376	2. 25.87	2. 360 miles
3. 404.9236	3. 13.77	3. 9.2 lbs.
4. 4002.65	4. 44.17	4. 438.77
5. 5209.1	5. 29.87	5. 22.5
6. 4955.2	6. 45.95	6. 4.59 miles
7. 4082.51	7. 27.19	7. $23
8. 2578.32	8. 47.29	8. 345 miles
9. 2953.76	9. 27.08	9. 1.92 lbs.
10. 1191.53	10. 14.98	10. 8
11. 268.9758	11. 12.56	11. 3.68 miles
12. 4707.61	12. 41.73	12. 100
13. 333.7985	13. 28.53	13. 390.1
14. 2062.43	14. 27.09	14. $60,000
15. 1603.26	15. 11.35	15. 258.5
16. 2228.09	16. 44.61	16. 12
17. 482.3511	17. 48.63	17. 107.5
18. 841.3015	18. 28.29	18. 696.14
19. 4900.91	19. 28.29	
20. 3150.93	20. 28.31	
21. 675.6404	21. 42.81	
22. 1200.81	22. 31.21	
23. 4349.01	23. 11.35	
24. 516.2817	24. 40.39	
25. 1013.27	25. 16.19	
26. 2177.4	26. 11.23	
27. 1376.1	27. 14.89	
28. 4621.81	28. 41.73	
29. 210.4555	29. 45.39	
30. 4231.33	30. 42.95	
31. 3822.31	31. 13.67	
32. 3079.53	32. 30.71	
33. 855.0851	33. 45.23	
34. 964.0246	34. 12.56	
35. 1566.97	35. 13.77	
36. 3320.82	36. 41.6	
37. 566.081	37. 42.95	
38. 1967.62	38. 44.17	
39. 3564.18	39. 29.5	
40. 4466.32	40. 44.02	

36.Dividend, Divisor, Quotient, and Remainder	31. Dividend 60	**37.Divide Whole Numbers by 1 Digit Numbers**
1. 7	31. Divisor 10	1. 15
3. 2	31. Quotient 6	2. 23
4. Dividend 32	32. 1	3. 18
4. Divisor 4	33. Dividend 30	4. 19
4. Quotient 8	33. Divisor 3	5. 17
5. 11	33. Quotient 10	6. 23
6. Dividend 44	34. Dividend 80	7. 16
6. Divisor 11	34. Divisor 8	8. 14
6. Quotient 4	34. Quotient 10	9. 21
7. 11	35. 5	10. 24
8. 2		11. 18
9. 6		12. 25
10. 4		13. 21
11. 8		14. 11
12. 5		15. 12
13. 13		16. 22
14. 10		17. 15
15. 4		18. 25
16. 3		19. 18
17. Dividend 30		20. 12
17. Divisor 5		21. 21
17. Quotient 6		22. 21
18. 70		23. 13
19. 15		24. 19
20. 3		25. 20
21. 12		26. 16
22. 4		27. 24
23. Dividend 72		28. 16
23. Divisor 9		29. 15
23. Quotient 8		30. 17
25. Dividend 24		31. 18
25. Divisor 6		32. 22
25. Quotient 4		33. 23
26. Dividend 84		34. 23
26. Divisor 7		35. 13
26. Quotient 12		36. 20
27. 9		37. 14
28. 4		38. 24
29. Dividend 24		39. 14
29. Divisor 2		40. 17
29. Quotient 12		
30. 44		

38.Divide Whole Numbers by 2 Digit Numbers	39.Divide Whole Numbers by 10, 100, 1000	40.Divide Whole Numbers Ending with Zero by 10, 100, 1000
1. 16	1. 7	1. 1200
2. 19	2. 11	2. 10
3. 18	3. 28	3. 9
4. 14	4. 9	4. 8
5. 18	5. 8	5. 11
6. 13	6. 11	6. 12
7. 14	7. 27	7. 230
8. 15	8. 26	8. 850
9. 12	9. 12	9. 48
10. 16	10. 253	10. 260
11. 11	11. 11	11. 29
12. 16	12. 252	12. 130
13. 13	13. 253	13. 1700
14. 16	14. 12	14. 390
15. 19	15. 8	15. 12
16. 12	16. 7	16. 140
17. 14	17. 251	17. 8
18. 19	18. 6	18. 1300
19. 15	19. 9	19. 760
20. 18	20. 10	20. 23
21. 15	21. 9	21. 2900
22. 11	22. 500	22. 320
23. 13	23. 8	23. 36
24. 17	24. 12	24. 150
25. 11	25. 28	25. 11
26. 18	26. 8	26. 47
27. 17	27. 10	27. 58
28. 19	28. 8	28. 10
29. 11	29. 251	29. 58
30. 18	30. 26	30. 130
31. 13	31. 6	31. 11
32. 19	32. 10	32. 1100
33. 12		
34. 15		
35. 17		
36. 17		
37. 13		
38. 14		
39. 18		
40. 11		

41.Division by 10s, 100s, 1000s	42.Simple Division (Word Problems)	43.Divide Whole Number by 1 Digit Number having Decimal Quotients
1. 10	1. 100	1. 22.5
2. 9	2. 10	2. 20.5
3. 2900	3. 5	3. 16.33
4. 47	4. 10	4. 12.25
5. 850	5. 15	5. 16.4
6. 23	6. 8	6. 12.17
7. 260	7. 10 min	7. 24.43
8. 12	8. 11	8. 17.5
9. 8	9. 10	9. 13.2
10. 48	10. 50	10. 17.33
11. 130	11. 10	11. 14.25
12. 11	12. 100 min	12. 16.5
13. 58	13. 20	13. 11.14
14. 11		14. 21.67
15. 29		15. 23.6
16. 11		16. 13.11
17. 1200		17. 20.67
18. 390		18. 14.2
19. 760		19. 15.17
20. 12		20. 14.17
21. 130		21. 14.14
22. 58		22. 20.29
23. 36		23. 12.5
24. 320		24. 19.5
25. 140		25. 11.11
26. 230		26. 24.75
27. 8		27. 13.14
28. 1300		28. 24.67
29. 150		29. 18.5
30. 10		30. 12.33
31. 1700		31. 25.38
32. 1100		32. 23.5
		33. 15.14
		34. 17.22
		35. 23.67
		36. 15.2
		37. 14.5
		38. 22.5
		39. 16.67
		40. 24.33

44.Divide Whole Number by 2 Digit Number having Decimal Quotients	45.Divide Whole Number by Whole Number having Remainder	
1. 14.4	1. 3	21. 3
2. 15.38	1. 2	21. 2
3. 16.5	2. 4	22. 4
4. 11.08	2. 2	22. 5
5. 13.25	3. 5	23. 4
6. 19.9	3. 4	23. 3
7. 17.58	4. 2	24. 5
8. 12.23	4. 4	24. 3
9. 13.19	5. 4	25. 3
10. 15.45	5. 5	25. 6
11. 19.53	6. 3	26. 3
12. 12.3	6. 5	26. 1
13. 16.55	7. 2	27. 5
14. 16.38	7. 4	27. 3
15. 11.06	8. 3	28. 3
16. 13.21	8. 4	28. 2
17. 15.42	9. 4	29. 5
18. 16.4	9. 6	29. 4
19. 11.09	10. 3	30. 2
20. 18.73	10. 6	30. 4
21. 12.25	11. 4	31. 5
22. 14.36	11. 6	31. 6
23. 16.46	12. 5	32. 4
24. 14.33	12. 6	32. 3
25. 19.69	13. 2	33. 4
26. 13.27	13. 1	33. 3
27. 18.57	14. 3	34. 5
28. 14.25	14. 1	34. 1
29. 17.47	15. 2	35. 4
30. 11.1	15. 5	35. 1
31. 12.21	16. 2	36. 4
32. 12.18	16. 5	36. 3
33. 11.07	17. 5	37. 2
34. 12.19	17. 2	37. 4
35. 13.3	18. 3	38. 5
36. 17.64	18. 4	38. 4
37. 18.53	19. 2	39. 4
38. 17.5	19. 1	39. 2
39. 11.08	20. 2	40. 4
40. 18.67	20. 6	40. 1

46.Divide Decimal Numbers by Whole Number having Decimal Quotients	47.Division Patterns	48.Division Problems (True or False)
1. 19.11	1. 500	1. False
2. 21.86	2. 2100	2. True
3. 15.92	3. 24000	3. False
4. 16.09	4. 1700	4. False
5. 18.27	5. 400	5. True
6. 13.61	6. 50	6. True
7. 26.07	7. 80	7. False
8. 15.67	8. 31000	8. False
9. 14.7	9. 27000	9. True
10. 26.99	10. 11000	10. False
11. 26.1	11. 40	11. True
12. 23.72	12. 4000	12. True
13. 17.18	13. 2000	13. True
14. 21.71	14. 100	14. False
15. 20.28	15. 1200	15. True
16. 20.45	16. 1800	16. False
17. 15.72	17. 29000	17. True
18. 21.34	18. 25000	18. False
19. 21.44	19. 6000	19. True
20. 17.13	20. 1500	20. False
21. 15.76	21. 30	21. False
22. 18.02	22. 90	22. False
23. 22.73	23. 800	23. True
24. 23.82	24. 1100	24. False
25. 12.46	25. 60	25. False
26. 12.65	26. 10000	26. False
27. 11.43	27. 1600	27. True
28. 11.56	28. 300	28. False
29. 21.54	29. 26000	29. False
30. 14.64	30. 30000	30. True
31. 15.73	31. 1400	31. False
32. 26.82	32. 2000	32. True
33. 24.98	33. 1000	33. False
34. 19.19	34. 20	34. False
35. 13.74	35. 7000	35. True
36. 26.91	36. 22000	36. True
37. 19.36	37. 200	37. False
38. 11.73	38. 900	38. False
39. 14.61	39. 70	39. True
40. 15.19	40. 600	40. False

49.Division Problems (Missing Number)
1. 5
2. 7
3. 4
4. 13
5. 1
6. 7
7. 4
8. 6
9. 12
10. 5
11. 8
12. 6
13. 5
14. 10
15. 8
16. 9
17. 5
18. 8
19. 6
20. 6
21. 3
22. 7
23. 2
24. 3
25. 4
26. 3
27. 2
28. 7
29. 8
30. 4
31. 5
32. 1
33. 12
34. 8
35. 8
36. 3
37. 9
38. 5
39. 2
40. 10

101Minute.com

Welcome to 101Minute.com, a guide dedicated to help students excel academically.

We are focused on creating educational programs that help to enhance student's skills across various grades and subjects. Modules are designed per grade level that progressively enhances their skill and confidence each day.

Each subject category has several quizzes designed to assess student's mastery with the concept. By consistently devoting 101 minutes per week, students can demonstrate significant improvement.

We are committed to serving our student community by building effective tools and reward programs. We are open to receiving feedback on how we can improve to make this an even better experience for our students. Our goal is to create a fun and learning social educational environment for students, and reward them for their achievements.

Please visit us at 101Minute.com.

Practice 101 Minutes Weekly to Master Your Math Skills

Made in the USA
Middletown, DE
03 November 2018